新东方
XDF.CN

MW01697953

新东方SAT/ACT课程指定用书

美国高考核心阅读

练习答案

新东方教育科技集团
国外考试推广管理中心 编著

浙江教育出版社·杭州

图书在版编目(CIP)数据

美国高考核心阅读 / 新东方教育科技集团国外考试推广管理中心编著. -- 杭州 : 浙江教育出版社, 2018.1
ISBN 978-7-5536-6273-2

Ⅰ. ①美… Ⅱ. ①新… Ⅲ. ①英语－阅读教学－高等学校－入学考试－美国－自学参考资料 Ⅳ. ①H319.37

中国版本图书馆CIP数据核字(2017)第216127号

美国高考核心阅读
MEIGUO GAOKAO HEXIN YUEDU
新东方教育科技集团国外考试推广管理中心 **编著**

责任编辑 罗 曼
美术编辑 韩 波
封面设计 李 倩
责任校对 马立改
责任印务 时小娟
版式设计 李 韬
出版发行 浙江教育出版社
地址：杭州市天目山路40号
邮编：310013
电话：(0571) 85170300 - 80928
邮箱：dywh@xdf.cn
网址：www.zjeph.com
印 刷 北京荣泰印刷有限公司
开 本 787mm×1092mm 1/16
成品尺寸 185mm×260mm
印 张 28.5
字 数 574 000
版 次 2018年1月第1版
印 次 2018年1月第1次印刷
标准书号 ISBN 978-7-5536-6273-2
定 价 78.00元(全两册)

CONTENTS / 目录

Chapter 1 | Passage 1

II. Text Structure

1. a general picture of transients in New York
2. the scene of a young man looking for a rented room and a housekeeper introducing him a vacant room
3. restless, shifting, fugacious
4. bleak and depressive
5. the young man asks the housekeeper whether a girl lived there
6. the young man rushes to ask the housekeeper but does not receive any useful information
7. the ebbing of his hope drained his faith
8. the young man's suicide
9. suicide
10. two housekeepers prattling over their beer about the death of a young woman in the room the previous week
11. the last sentence

III. Character Analysis

The tenant, a young man

The young man, remaining nameless throughout the article, conveys the image of a transient who rushes to a big city for his lost lover but finds nothing but isolation and hopelessness.

He is a typical transient, as described in the first paragraphs. He wears a hat and carries the hand-baggage, just as transients "carry their lares et penates in a bandbox; their vine is entwined about a picture hat." In this sense, his experience could be the one any transient is or will have, and his ending could be the one any transient could choose.

He loves the girl deeply. The love supports his ceaseless search for her for five months, from high-class theaters to humble music halls, from schools to houses for renting.

He is lonely, vulnerable and depressed. Five months' search smothers his hope, leading to his suicide.

Mrs. Purdy, the housekeeper

The lady, upon her first appearance, impresses the reader with a negative image of "an unwholesome, surfeited worm." The detailed description of the worm implies her greed for she "now sought to fill the vacancy with edible lodgers."

She looks professional, introducing her room with a detailed, precise description of its facilities and tenants. She seems hospitable, answering the young man's question about his girl with elaborate answers.

But actually she is a cold-hearted, selfish liar. She tells the young tenant over and again that no girl with a mole by her left eyebrow, as he describes, lived in the room. However, during the small talk with another housekeeper at the end of the story, she admits that she did not tell him a girl with the mole killed herself in that room, because she did not want to lose his rent. Mrs. Purdy has won. She receives the young man's pay for a week in advance, before he goes back to the awful room and commits suicide.

She might be said to be the antagonist of the story, who symbolizes the greedy, pitiless city of New York—or any other big city in the world.

Eloise Vashner, the young man's girlfriend

The girl never shows up in the story physically, but readers can figure out from the description about her a story that a town girl moved to a monstrous city for making her actress dream come true, but ended up in a rented room where she kills herself with gas.

She might love the young man, since she had called him "dear." But she might not love him, since she left no trace for him to search for.

She must wear mignonette-smelled perfume so that the young man might search crazily for what she might have left in the room, after smelling "the strong, sweet odour of mignonette."

She must wear a black satin hair-bow, for the young man halted, "poised between ice and fire," when finding such a hair bow in a drawer.

She must be brave, since she had moved to a strange city alone, where she knew no one and no one knew her. But she must not be brave enough, for she did not survive in this indifferent city, where no one, except the housekeeper, remembered her.

IV. Theme

1. D   2. C   3. E   4. B   5. A

V. Rhetorical Analysis

1.

修辞 oxymoron

分析 How can homeless people have a hundred homes? Actually, these people do not have real homes, but just flit between furnished rooms. The oxymoron reveals their tragic lives full of instability and turbulence.

翻译 他们无家可归，却又有上百个家。

2.

修辞 personification; simile

分析 The room is given some human attributes so that the reader may gain a better understanding of the atmosphere in the room. The "welcome" is compared to "the specious smile of a demirep." A demirep, or a whore, would only welcome her guests with fake hospitality, so the reader could imagine that the room is not welcoming at all.

翻译 客房以假惺惺的热情迎接新到的客人，像暗娼脸上堆起的假笑，红中透病，面容憔悴，马马虎虎。

3.

修辞 metaphor

分析 The word "ebbing" suggests that the young man is losing his hope, just as waves are on the ebb. The loss of hope also brings his faith away, leading to his suicide in the end.

翻译 消退的希望让他的信心丧失殆尽。

4.

修辞 allusion

分析 The place where the worm dieth seldom is the hell, according to the Bible. The allusion suggests that the mansion is the hell and the housekeepers are the devil.

翻译 麦克库尔夫人和珀迪夫人在一个地下休息室所坐了下来。这是房东们聚会、蛆虫猖獗的地方。

VI. Language and Style

6.1 Language Focus

6.1.1 Inversion Drills

1. A　　2. C　　3.B　　4. B　　5.B

6.1.2 Semicolon Drills

1. A 考查内容：带逗号的长并列成分可以用分号隔开。
2. C 考查内容：在连接两个独立完整句的连接副词或过渡性短语之前，才会使用分号。
3. A 考查内容：在连接两个独立完整句的连接副词或过渡性短语之前使用分号。
4. B 考查内容：在连接两个独立完整句的连接副词或过渡性短语之前使用分号。

6.2 Language Analysis

1.

语法标签 并列句，表语从句，主语从句

翻　译 壁里面也许放过圣人像，但是不难想象，黑暗中大大小小的魔鬼已经把圣人拽入黑暗，拽到下面某间带家具的房间那邪恶的深渊中。

2.

语法标签 并列句，表语从句，现在分词短语

翻　译 他确信，自从她从家乡消失后，这个水流环绕的大城市就一直把她藏在某处，但它也像一团巨大的流沙，沙粒的位置不停变换，没有根基，今天还浮在表层的细粒明天就被淤泥和黏土覆盖到下面去了。

3.

语法标签 现在分词短语，形容词短语，宾语从句，状语从句

翻　译 他像一条追寻气味的猎犬，在房间里四处搜寻，环视四壁，趴在地上仔细察看拱起垫子的每个角落，搜遍了壁炉台和桌子、帘子和幔帐，以及角落里东倒西歪的橱柜；他想找到一个清晰可见的痕迹，但没能找到迹象表明她就在他身旁、四周、对面、心中、上方，或是紧紧地缠着他、诱惑着他，并通过他比较敏锐的感官部分发出辛酸的呼唤，以至于即使是他较愚钝的感官部分也能认出这是她发出的呼唤声……他什么也没找到。

6.3 Style and Tone

1. third-person　2. bleak and depressive　3. imagery / sensory language
4. chronological　5. sympathy

VII. Exercises

7.1 Vocabulary

1. D	2. F	3. A	4. E	5. C	
6. B	7. J	8. K	9.G	10. H	11. I

7.2 Text Comprehension

1. There are many paragraphs which reveal the young man's personality. For example, line 62-67 reveals his thought after he failed to find the girl after five months. "He was sure... in ooze and slime." suggests that he is somewhat pessimistic, since it is impossible to find upper granules of today and tomorrow. He is also loyal, for line 84-85 reads, "he would recognize the smallest thing that had belonged to her or that she had touched."
2. In line 18-20, the housekeeper is compared to "an unwholesome, surfeited worm that had eaten its nut to a hollow shell and now sought to fill the vacancy with edible lodgers." The metaphor suggests that housekeepers might stand for those who only care for money, without any sympathy for their tenants. The suggestion is also justified by the chat between the two housekeepers at the end of the story.
3. The housekeeper's words in line 43-46 and line 54-56 show that the life of theater people is constantly changing since they come and go quickly. This implies that Miss Eloise Vashner

might live the same life. And she could not be famous in the city, since the young tenant searched all theaters, high or low-class, but in vain. Therefore, it may be inferred that she killed herself because she might not bear the life or her anonymousness.

4. In line 67-69, the room is described as "a demirep" with a hectic, haggard, perfunctory welcome. It indicates that the room may stand for the atmosphere in the city which actually does not welcome transients but pretends to do so. Moreover, line 109-110 shows that the room was dead when the young tenant crept back to it, getting no clue about the girl's whereabouts. Consequently, the room could also represent hope.
5. The housekeeper would ask the other housekeeper to help her move the dead out, just as the latter says in line 134-135: "I' is just one wake ago this day I helped ye lay out the third floor, back." And she would not inform the next tenant of the news, just as she does to the young man.

II. Text Structure

1. starts running as fast as he can in the direction of the mining camp
2. optimistic
3. ashamed
4. has a vision of himself with his crowd of buddies discovering his own body the next day
5. warned him against traveling alone
6. waits for a while
7. howls for a few moments
8. it will find food and a fire

III. Character Analysis

The man

In the beginning of the story, the man, or the protagonist, has blind confidence in himself, believing that he could beat nature, as shown in line 11-12 "Maybe, if he continued to run, his feet would stop freezing. Maybe if he ran far enough, he would find the camp and the boys." Also, he ignored advice from the old man of Sulphur Creek before he travels alone (inferred from line 74-75). When facing death, however, he finally develops some awe for nature and accepts his fate, as in line 61-62 "Freezing was not as bad as people thought. There were many worse ways to die." In this way, nature can be taken as the antagonist.

The dog

The dog is a major character, who follows the man closely, but we can see from its three contacts with the man (line 6, line 45-47, and line 77-84) that it may not be friends with the man. It stays with him only for survival for its instinct tells it that mankind can make a fire in the snow. Once it finds that the man cannot build a fire, it leaves him without hesitation for "other food providers and fire providers." (line 89)

The old man from Sulfur Creek

From the very brief description of the old man ("warm, comfortable, and smoking a pipe", line 72-73), we may infer that he is quite calm. He is also wise enough to respect nature, for he warned the man of the danger before the man travels along the creek bed (inferred from line 74-75).

The boys (the friends waiting in the camp)

It is hard to figure out the boys' personality, since they only come in the middle (line 26) and at the end (line 63-68) and have no physical appearance in the story. They could stand for civilization, since they wait at the camp, where there is food and, most importantly, fire. They may be considered as the man's friends or helpers, since the man thinks about going back to them and has the delusion that they would look for him.

IV. Theme

1. D 2. C 3. A 4. B

V. Rhetorical Analysis

1.

修辞 imagery

分析 Visual imagery here reveals to the reader the same sight that the protagonist sees. It would appeal to the reader's empathy, giving them the feeling that they were there.

翻译 慢慢地，当他挣扎着穿过雪堆的时候，他重新开始看见河岸、枝桠光秃的树木和天空。

2.

修辞 simile

分析 Through the simile, the reader would sense the man's despair and foresee his doomed fate.

翻译 他一直飞奔着，像一只被砍了头的鸡。

3.

修辞 contrast

分析 This obvious contrast between "brief" and "long", "day" and "evening" is written to create a special effect: for nature, it is just a short day, or one of numerous days; but for the man, it is a long evening, during which he struggles for his life for quite a time.

翻译 短暂的白天结束，漫长的黑夜降临。

4.

修辞 personification

分析 Stars are given human attributes here. Despite the man's death, they behave cheerfully—"leaped and danced and shone brightly." The indifference of the stars actually discloses the theme that could be found in all Jack London's short stories - nature is indifferent to humans.

翻译 狗又逗留了一会，星星在凄冷的天空中跳跃着、舞蹈着、明亮地闪烁着，而它对着星星发出了一阵长嚎。

VI. Language and Style

6.1 Language Focus

1. D 2. B 3. A 4. C 5. B

6. C 7. A 8. A 9. C 10. A

6.2 Language Analysis

1.

语法标签 时间状语从句，冒号

翻　　译 他想一直跑到营地、跑到那些人面前的计划有一个漏洞，那就是他没有那样的耐力。

2.

语法标签 宾语从句，定语从句

翻　　译 然后男人坠入了在他看来自己经历过的最舒服、最满意的一场梦里。

3.

语法标签 定语从句，并列句

翻　　译 然后，它转过身，朝着它所知道的营地的方向在河道上跑了起来，那还有其他能够提供食物和火的人。

6.3 Style and Tone

1. his protagonist
2. harsh, natural
3. naturalism
4. Imagery
5. a life-and-death struggle with nature
6. Simile, personification

VII. Exercises

7.1 Vocabulary

1. D 2. C 3. E 4. A 5. B

7.2. Text Comprehension

1. The man symbolizes the human race, who always believes that man can defeat nature. Driven by the belief, humans often ignore warnings from nature and try their luck in nature. They may end up in a fatal tragedy.
2. The dog represents pure instinct, a trait necessary for survival in the harsh Yukon. Unlike the man, who requires the products of intellectual civilization—warm clothing, matches, maps, thermometers—the dog simply uses its own natural advantages—fur and a keen sense of smell. Perhaps more importantly, the dog has an instinctive understanding of the cold. It knows that such conditions are dangerous and unsuitable for traveling alone; it follows the man closely, just with the belief that he can bulid a fire which defends them against the

freezing weather. This sense of instinct preserves the dog as opposed to the man—it even knows instinctively when the man is attempting to kill it (to warm his hands in its carcass). Although the dog cannot create a fire for itself, or even hunt down food in the wild so well, its instinct keeps it alive and allows it to find the nearby camp of men.

London introduces the dog to act as a foil to the main character, that is, the dog has key differences that contrast sharply with the man, such as its physical features and its instinct. By showing how the dog reacts to events in the story, London further highlights the man's inexperience and the seriousness of his situation.

3. Line 24-25 reads, "He seemed to be flying along above the surface and to have no connection with the earth."
4. When the man is dying, he recalls the old man's words and murmurs, "You are right." From his words, it could be deducted that the old-timers could have warned the man of the danger of traveling alone in such a cold place as the Yukon.
5. There is no need to name the man or the dog, since they symbolize man and animal. By not naming the characters, London has also placed the man at an even greater distance from the reader within his deadly setting, thus isolating him all the more in a bleak and hostile universe.

Passage 3

II. Text Structure

1. the Ceremony of Twelve
2. bicycle
3. hard
4. committee
5. Nobody
6. the Elders
7. Lily
8. uncertain
9. nervous

III. Character Analysis

1. Jonas doubts the decisions made by the Elders since he asked his father "were any of the Elevens disappointed, your year"(line 80). This question shows that Jonas thought the Assignment could not make everyone happy.
2. The father thought that it was doubtless that the Assignment made by the Elders was always right. This could be inferred from the answer he made to Jonas's question about whether there was somebody disappointed by the Assignment—"No, I don't think so. Of course the Elders are so careful in their observations and selections."
3. It can be inferred that the mother was devoted to her work and the Community, because she was convinced that everything the Elders did was right.

IV. Theme

The theme of this passage is uncertainty, worry and doubt, which is shown by the questions (about the unreasonable rules in the society) Jonas raises for his father.

VI. Language and Style

6.1 Language Analysis

1.

语法标签 破折号

分　析 此处双破折号之间的部分是插入语，起补充信息（additional information）的作用

翻　译 嗯，我很清楚——后来我的父母告诉我，他们也很清楚——我的倾向和才能是什么。

2.

语法标签 破折号

分析 此处破折号表示话被打断。

翻译 当我的朋友们在比谁骑车更快，或者用他们的建筑玩具做玩具汽车或桥，或者——

3.

语法标签 破折号

分析 此处表示语气的停顿。

翻译 嗯，有个叫 Andrei 的——我记得当时我们还小，他从不喜欢做活动。

6.2 Style and Tone

1. C 2. A 3. A

VII. Exercises

7.1 Vocabulary

1. govern 2. thrill 3. suspense 4. affectionate
5. drew 6. release 7. shivered 8. imaginary
9. C 10. C 11. B

7.2. Text Comprehension

1. F 2. F 3. T 4. F 5. F
6. Those comfort objects are used to comfort babies when they are first adopted by strangers, the family units in this utopian society, since they are too young to get used to a totally different environment from the Nurturing Center.
7. The Ceremony of Twelve will be the day when the Elders assign the lifelong task for citizens who are among the Twelves. It represents change.
8. The Receiver might be an Elder of the highest social status. He should be very important in and respected by the society. There is no clue about his jobs and responsibilities in this society, but they must be very different from those of the Elders.

Chapter 1 Passage 4

II. Text Structure

1. a little girl driving home her cow
2. the town to the countryside
3. the young ornithologist
4. he is an ornithologist
5. hunt, kill, and stuff birds for his pleasure
6. her grandmother's farm
7. a rare white heron
8. take the adventure to find the bird for the young man
9. the heron, its nest, and its mate
10. guards her secret

III. Character Analysis

1. C 2. B 3. D 4. D 5. B

6. grandmother
7. noisy manufacturing town
8. hunter
9. friendship or romantic love
10. does not
11. "determined, and somewhat aggressive"
12. ten dollars
13. romantic love
14. four
15. far away

IV. Theme

1. freedom 2. emancipation 3. industrialism
4. industrialization 5. individual human being

V. Rhetorical Analysis

1.

修辞 simile

分析 将干裂的树枝比作愤怒地抓她的爪子，simile 是明喻，关键词为 like。

翻译 路比她预料的要难走；她得爬得再高些，抓得再紧些。尖锐干裂的树枝像愤怒的爪般抓住她、缠着她、划伤她；她抱着树干慢慢地向上爬，树干把她单薄瘦小的小手蹂躏得十分粗糙、僵硬。

2.

修辞 personification

分析 大树在沉睡，是将大树拟人化

翻译 那棵参天大树仍沉睡在苍白的月光下。瘦小的、傻乎乎的 Sylvia 鼓起最大勇气爬到树顶。热烈翻腾的血液贯穿她整个身体，她赤裸着的手脚如鸟爪一般紧紧抓住庞大的梯子般的树干向上攀爬，几乎要触及天际。

3.

修辞 imagery, simile 和 shift from third-person-limited point of view to second-person-point of view。

分析 直接与 Sylvia 对话，将登高后望见白鹭的场景热情洋溢地推向高潮。

翻译 现在再往下看，Sylvia，在那闪光的白桦和黑色的铁杉之间的绿色沼泽上；在那里你会再一次见到你曾见过的白鹭；看啊，看啊！他像一个白点，如一片漂浮的羽毛般从一片死寂的黑铁杉间窜出，变大了，飞高了，最终靠近了；他稳稳地扑闪的翅膀，伸展开纤细的脖子和戴着勋章般的，稳稳地掠过针叶林。

4.

修辞 sensory

分析 利用听觉感官（heard the echo of his whistle）来表达 Sylvia 的思念。

翻译 Sylvia 在无数个赶着悠闲得赶着奶牛回家的夜晚里，仿佛听到他的哨声飘荡在这条原野的小路上。

VI. Language Analysis

1.

语法标签 倒装，定语从句

翻　　译 盐沼地在不远处的海这边，它在 Sylvia 心里萦绕着，她一直想看，但从来没有见过。有时在风暴的夜里，海的声音盖过了森林的声音，传到耳里。

2.

语法标签 倒装

翻　　译 在这些鹰、蝙蝠、飞蛾，甚至是歌唱的画眉之外的，是一个有灰色眼睛的孤独的小女孩勇敢而跳动的心。

3.

语法标签 分词，名词性从句

翻　　译 Tilley 夫人饶有兴趣地听着这些，但是 Sylvia 不像她平时的样子，似乎对此全未察觉，她仍然盯着那只想要钻进门阶下洞的癞蛤蟆。

4.

语法标签 虚拟语气

翻　　译 所有人都说，对一个在拥挤的工业城市里生活了八年的小女孩来说，这是个挺大的改变。但是，对 Sylvia 自己来说，她感觉在来到农场之前，自己似乎没有存在过。

VII. Exercises

7.1 Vocabulary

1. provoking	2. for all	3. consolation	4. zest	5. torment
6. quaint	7. elusive	8. ceased	9. hastening	10. perch

7.2 Text Comprehension

1. F 2. F 3.T 4. F 5. F

Chapter 1 Passage 5

II. Text Structure

1. inspirations 2. great letter writer

III. Theme

talent and admiration. The author expressed her admiration for Horace Walpole's great talent as a letter writer.

IV. Rhetorical Analysis

1.

修辞 rhetorical question

分析 此处有两个反问。反问的作用是加强语气，把本已确定的观点（Macaulay 和 Tennyson 在这两个方面的权威；作者无法随心所欲地从 impersonal stare 转回 little circle）变得更加鲜明强烈、不容置疑。

翻译 有谁能写出比 Macaulay 更精彩的政党历史，又有谁能描绘出比 Tennyson 更细腻的景色风光？但注视着他们的正是此刻——贪婪的普罗众生；如此一来，作家如何能够随心所愿地在睽睽众目下转身，仅只面对房间里的寥寥数人呢？

2.

修辞 analogy

分析 此处把写信之于 Macaulay 与化妆之于女演员建立联系，在理解的难度上化繁为简，化抽象晦涩为生动具体，能够引起读者的阅读兴趣，并能使其更好地理解作者观点。

翻译 就算是写信给自己的亲姐妹，Macaulay 仍是采用面对公众读者的写作方式，就好像女演员无法把脸上的脂粉抹掉，自然地坐在桌边喝茶一样。

3.

修辞 rhetorical question

分析 反问是用疑问表达确定的修辞手法，作用是加强语气。

翻译 那么，这种高尚艺术在 19 世纪的衰落，是不是愈发有利可图的文学创作和愈发关心赚钱的作家们共同导致的结果呢？

4.

修辞 metonymy

分析 使用借喻的修辞手法时，本体不出现，喻体直接代替本体。此处喻体是 owl 和 ghoul，本体是 the public。由于只有喻体出现，所以在使用借喻的修辞手法时，文章能产生更加深厚、含蓄的表达效果，同时语言也更加简洁。

翻译 而 Tennyson 对大众的恐惧——“当我活着的时候，猫头鹰监视着我；而我死了，就成了恶鬼们的大餐”——使得他仅留下少量所有人都能看到的干巴巴的笔记，或被出版成书，或被博物馆收集，放在玻璃柜子里任人阅读。

5.

修辞 rhetorical question, parallelism, antithesis

分析 反问的作用是加强语气，把本已确定的观点（something superficial yet profound, something changing yet entire 的就是 Horace Walpole 他自己）变得更加鲜明强烈，不容置疑。

对立内容：superficial vs. profound, changing vs entire 这两种修辞手法叠加后产生了加强语气的作用。形式上，这一组表达结构整齐，具有音律美；内容上，它的精简凝练，通过两组意思相反的词语制造出了冲突的效果，加强了语言的表现力。

翻译 从这些信中，他的朋友们能够了解的除了那些才华横溢的观点、趣闻轶事、对化装舞会和午夜狂欢场景的生动描述之外，还有一些虽浮于表面却意义重大的东西，一些变化着的却又攸关全局的东西——他自己。在缺乏恰当的语言去描述的时候，我们能否这么去命名这些在朋友面前可以显现却无法被公众接受的东西呢？

V. Language and Style

5.1 Language Analysis

1.

语法标签 倒装结构

分　析 此处主语是 his immortality，谓语是 sprang，由于状语前置，导致了主谓倒装。

翻　译 他的不朽由此而来。

2.

语法标签 倒装结构；破折号

分　析 倒装句：Looking them full in the face was the present moment. 此处主语是 the present moment，谓语部分是 was looking，本句是主谓倒装的结构。此处破折号的作用是解释说明，把 the present moment 解释为 the great gluttonous public。

翻　译 但注视着他们的正是此刻——贪婪的普罗众生；如此一来，作家如何能够随心所愿地在睽睽众目下转身，仅只面对房间里的寥寥数人呢？

3.

语法标签 强调句

分　析 本句话中的强调结构为 was it...that，强调的部分是 the growth of writing as a paid profession, and the change which that change of focus brought with it。

翻　译 那么，这种高尚艺术在 19 世纪的衰落，是不是愈发有利可图的文学创作和愈发关心赚钱的作家们共同导致的结果呢？

4.

语法标签 宾语从句前置

分　析 本句为宾语从句前置结构，语序可以整理为：But the letters themselves with their perpetual variety deny that he allowed the featureless face of posterity to stand between him and the very voice and dress of his friends, how they looked and how they thought。

翻　译 但是，从内容上看，这些涉及各个领域的信件又可以否定 Walpole 在创作时考虑到了后代子孙，让这些平平的普罗大众站在他和友人之间，去观察他们的样子，了解他们的思想。

5.2 Style and Tone

1. C　　2. A　　3. A　　4. A　　5. B

VI. Exercises

6.1 Vocabulary

1. incessant　　2. winds　　3. surreptitious　　4. pompous
5. elicit　　6. exquisite　　7. decline　　8. stagnate
9. A　　10. C　　11. B　　12. B　　13. C

6.2 Text Comprehension

1. F　　2. F　　3.F　　4. T　　5. F

6. **Claims:**

In the first paragraph, the author makes the claim that Walpole wrote not only for friends, but for posterity. He uses several reasons to develop this claim.

Reasons:

He had meant to write the history of his own times.

After twenty years he gave it up, and decided to write another kind of history—a history ostensibly inspired by friends but in fact written for posterity.

But that he allowed the featureless face of posterity to stand between him and the very voice and dress of his friends, how they looked and how they thought, the letters themselves with their perpetual variety deny.

He cannot keep the pompous, style any longer, nor mend a careless phrase, and so, flexible as an eel, he winds from high politics to living faces and the past and its memories—

7. The author thinks that the art of letter writing reveals about the vitalizing role of real letters in our lives: not only for private contact, but for recording the history from different point of views. Woolf points out the power of the letter, which bridges two privacies, in assuring us of our own selves, since the writer could stay in his own little circle and write whatever he really wants, without being stared by the public.

Chapter 2 Passage 1

II. Text Structure

1. public knowledge 2. disagreement 3. transformation
4. contradicting 5. determines 6. indirect

III. Argument Analysis

1. A 2. C

V. Language Focus

5.1 Language Focus

5.1.1 Pronoun Drills

1. D 考查内容：指代混淆——their 此处指代了科学家们
2. B 考查内容：代词形式须与先行词一致
3. A 考查内容：代词形式须与先行词一致
4. B 考查内容：代词形式须与先行词一致
5. B 考查内容：代词形式须与先行词一致

5.1.2 Comma Drills

1. A 考查内容：两个以上名词并列
2. D 考查内容：两个以上名词并列
3. C 考查内容：过渡性短语
4. B 考查内容：过渡性短语
5. C 考查内容：过渡性短语
6. B 考查内容：非限定性定语从句接在主句后时，需要用逗号隔开
7. B 考查内容：从句前置时，要用逗号把它和主句分隔开
8. B 考查内容：逗号和并列连词连接两个完整句

5.2 Language Analysis

1.

语法标签 定语从句

分　析 Whereby 引导定语从句时，可以看作 by which

翻　译 在权威转变的过程中，人们开始批判地接受公共知识，要求所有权威阐明是什么价值观左右了新闻内容的决策。

2.

语法标签 省略句

分　析 原句 the latest news a mere fleeting episode in a relentless process of revision and re-description of reality 省略了谓语 can be。

翻　译 在这种环境下，公共知识不稳定是必然的，最新消息只是这种无情地修改和重述真实的过程中的一个短暂片段罢了。

VI. Exercises

6.1 Vocabulary

1. circulation	2. provisional	3. oblique	4. relentless
5. rival	6. slanted	7. parity	8. bluster
9. B	10. A	11. A	

6.2 Text Comprehension

1. F　2. T　3. F　4. F　5. T

5. The general public call for a transformation of authority from the center of news production to the citizens themselves, while journalists hold the opposite point of view.
6. People question the whole news production industry, instead of journalists; moreover, the public still trust some media and type of stories. Therefore, people do not express their distrust directly.

Chapter 2 Passage 2

I. Warm Up

1.3.1 Skimming

1. Three
2. The third mode—wealth can be administered during their lives by its possessors.

II. Text Structure

Paragraph 1

The author starts with a general statement in this paragraph, "There are but three modes in which surplus wealth can be disposed of. It call be left to the families of the decedents; or it can be bequeathed for public purposes; or, finally, it can be administered during their lives by its possessors."

He proceeds to comment on the first mode and claims it "the most injudicious." Further, he employs two paralleled examples, situations in both monarchical countries and republican institutions, to illustrate this point of view.

Paragraph 2

The author continues the discussion on the first mode of wealth distribution in this paragraph.

Paragraph 3

The author starts to assess on the second mode of wealth distribution in this paragraph, saying that wealth is not supposed to achieve its purpose posthumously. He primarily relies on reasoning and counterexamples to support his point of view.

Paragraph 4

The author continues the discussion on the second mode and makes further comment claiming it "condemnation of the selfish millionaire's unworthy life."

Paragraph 5 & 6

The author continues the discussion on other possibilities deriving from the second mode.

Paragraph 7

The author draws the conclusion in this paragraph that only the third mode would work out the imbalanced distribution of property.

III. Argument Analysis

Paragraph 1 & 2

The author introduces the general statement at the beginning of the article: "There are but three modes in which surplus wealth can be disposed of. It call be left to the families of the decedents; or it can be bequeathed for public purposes; or, finally, it can be administered during their lives by its possessors."

Then the author makes his first claim—the first is the most injudicious.

The author uses several rhetorical questions to support his claim that it is unwise to leave wealth to heirs: "Why should men leave great fortunes to their children?" and "If this is done from affection, is it not misguided affection?" He also reasons that "observation teaches that, generally speaking, it is not well for the children that they should be so burdened. Neither is it well for the state."

As to evidence, the author employs three examples that either in monarchical countries, or in Great Britain, or under republican institutions, leaving large sums of money to heirs causes more harm than good to support his claim.

Moreover, the author anticipates possible objection that "It is not suggested that men who have failed to educate their sons to earn a livelihood shall cast them adrift in poverty." He concedes that "If any man has seen fit to rear his sons with a view to their living idle lives, or, what is highly commendable, has instilled in them the sentiment that they are in a position to labor for public ends without reference to pecuniary considerations, then, of course, the duty of the parent is to see that such are provided for." However, he counters the prospect with a metaphor that "such are the very salt of the earth, as valuable as, unfortunately, they are rare."

Paragraph 3 & 4

The author makes his second claim that "knowledge of the results of legacies bequeathed is not calculated to inspire the brightest hopes of much posthumous good being accomplished" to dispute the second mode of wealth distribution.

To substantiate his claim, he lists several reasons: first, "it is well to remember that it requires the exercise of not less ability than that which acquired the wealth to use it so as to be really beneficial to the community;" second, "besides this, it may fairly be said that no man is to be extolled for doing what he cannot help doing, nor is he to be thanked by the community to which he only leaves wealth at death."

In regard to evidence, the author employs a counterexample that "the cases are not few in which the real object sought by the testator is not attained, nor are they few in which his real wishes are thwarted."

To make his claim more reasonable, he raises another possibility "the growing disposition to tax more and more heavily large estates left at death" as the examples in the State of Pennsylvania and the British Parliament. But he also provides a counterargument to dispute such alternatives that "by taxing estates heavily at death the state marks its condemnation of the selfish millionaire's unworthy life."

Paragraph 6

The author makes the third claim in the sixth paragraph that "this policy would work powerfully to induce the rich man to attend to the administration of wealth during his life, which is the end that society should always have in view, as being that by far most fruitful for the people."

To support this claim, he reasons that "nor need it be feared that this policy would sap the root of enterprise and render men less anxious to accumulate, for to the class whose ambition it is to leave great fortunes and be talked about after their death, it will attract even more attention, and, indeed, be a somewhat nobler ambition to have enormous sums paid over to the state from their fortunes."

Paragraph 7

After the author contradicts the first two mode of wealth distribution with reasons and examples, he safely draws the conclusion that "here remains, then, only one mode of using great fortunes; but in this we have the true antidote for the temporary unequal distribution of wealth, the reconciliation of the rich and the poor."

He provides three reasons to explain why he lends full supports to this mode: first, "it is founded upon the present most intense individualism, and the race is projected to put it in practice by degree whenever it pleases;" second, "under its sway we shall have an ideal state, in which the surplus wealth of the few will become, in the best sense the property of the many, because administered for the common good, and this wealth, passing through the hands of the few, can be made a much more potent force for the elevation of our race than if it had been distributed in small sums to the people themselves;" third, "even the poorest can be made to see this, and to agree that great sums gathered by some of their fellow-citizens and spent for public purposes, from which the masses reap the principal benefit, are more valuable to them than if scattered among them through the course of many years in trifling amounts."

IV. Rhetorical Analysis

修辞 metaphor

分析 The author compares the enterprise of the men undertaking as a tree, and fears not that the policy would sap the root of the enterprise.

翻译 不必担忧的是，此政策并不会使富人的事业行将就木，也不会挫败他们积攒财富的决心，因为富人阶级的追求在于留下大量财富并且在死后被人谈论，这将会吸引更多的注意，甚至作为更高尚的追求把巨大的财富交付给国家。

V. Language and Style

5.1 Language Focus

5.1.1 Parenthetical Drills

1. A 考查内容：非必要性的插入语成分和必要的句子谓语成分的区别
2. B 考查内容：用破折号连接的同位语
3. B 考查内容：混淆句子必要成分和同位语
4. A 考查内容：插入语
5. A 考查内容：逗号隔开名词同位语

5.1.2 Dash Drills

1. C 考查内容：双破折号内为同位语成分
2. B 考查内容：破折号内为非限定成分，起列举解释作用
3. C 考查内容：易混淆的情况（误以为强调句的 that 部分为转折或总结）
4. A 考查内容：双破折号强调同位语
5. B 考查内容：essentially 作副词，修饰整个句子。a tool 是 is 的表语，中间不使用标点符号。

5.2 Language Analysis

1.

语法标签 同位语从句，条件状语从句

分　析 If any man has seen fit to rear his sons with a view to their living idle lives, or, what is highly commendable, has instilled in them the sentiment that they are in a position to labor for public ends without reference to pecuniary considerations, then, of course, the duty of the parent is to see that such are provided for.

翻　译 如果有人认为养儿育女是要让他们过上安逸的生活，更让人钦佩的是，要把不为私利服务社群的观念灌输给子女，当然，父母的责任便是如此。

2.

语法标签 并列结构

分　析 ...The thoughtful man must shortly say, “I would as soon leave to my son a curse as the almighty dollar,” and admit to himself that it is not the welfare of the children but family pride which inspires these enormous legacies.

翻　译 这种例子，不幸的是，极其珍贵，也极其罕有。同时，毫无意外的定律便是，当人看着自己的遗产行将赠予受益人的时候，不得不感慨：“这巨额遗产无疑对我后世来说只是个诅咒。”同时，不得不承认的是，遗产对孩子来说并不是福利，只是为了满足家族虚荣，而将巨额遗产予以相赠。

3.

语法标签 定语从句，并列结构

分　析 Men, who continue hoarding great sums all their lives, the proper use of which—for public ends would work good to the community, should be made to feel that the community, in the form of the state, cannot thus be deprived of its proper share.

翻　译 富人，一生都在兢兢业业积攒财富；而财富的有效使用，应当用于社区，惠泽于社区，这样才不枉其功。

4.

语法标签 并列句式，后置定语

分　析 There remains, then, only one mode of using great fortunes ; but in this we have the true antidote for the temporary unequal distribution of wealth, the reconciliation of the rich and the poor—a reign of harmony—another ideal, differing, indeed, from that of the Communist in requiring only the further evolution of existing conditions, not the total overthrow of our civilization.

翻　译 如此，便只剩下一种财富分配的方式；但是，此模式却是暂时解决财富分配不均的解药，调解穷人与富人之间的矛盾，使之趋之和谐；这一理想状态，并不会颠覆现有的文明，更有别于共产主义的方式，因共产主义只会不断变革现有的制度。

5.3 Style and Tone

1. monarchical countries		2. republic institutions	
3. the State of Pennsylvania		4. the British Parliament	
5. 1	6. 1	7. 2	8. 3
9. 4	10. first	11. second	12. third

VI. Exercises

6.1 Vocabulary

1. C	2. E	3.B	4. A	5. F	6.D

6.2 Text Comprehension

1. Leaving large sums of wealth to offspring proves to be futile either in monarchical countries or in republican institutions. The author questions that leaving great fortunes to children is misguided affection. He claims that large fortunes burden children, working more for injury than good.
2. First, legacies bequeathed are not calculated to achieve posthumous good. Cases are not few that real object of the legacies is not attained, and even the real wishes are thwarted. Second, it

requires the exercise of not less ability than that which acquired the wealth to use it so as to be really beneficial to the community.

3. First, the policy will work powerfully to encourage rich people to attend to the administration of wealth during their lives. It will not sap the root of enterprise or discourage men to accumulate wealth. Second, the policy is founded upon the most intense individualism, and the race is projected to put it in practice by degree whenever it pleases.
4. It is founded upon the present most intense individualism, and the race is projected to put it in practice by degree whenever it pleases. Under its sway we shall have an ideal state, in which the surplus wealth of the few will become, in the best sense the property of the many, because administered for the common good, and this wealth, passing through the hands of the few, can be made a much more potent force for the elevation of our race than if it had been distributed in small sums to the people themselves.

Passage 3

II. Text Structure

1. Young Americans have lost their zest for cars.
2. The HCDT report
3. lifestyles and values
4. the Internet
5. We simply don't know yet.

III. Argument Analysis

1. reasons
2. economic factors
3. the high unemployment
4. meager wage gains of the Great Recession
5. on-demand transportation services
6. a quotation from Forbes magazine
7. the fact of car pollution
8. the fact that both cars and the Internet are social instruments
9. too much traffic congestion
10. the car culture thrives rather than withers

IV. Rhetorical Analysis

1.

修辞 personification

分析 The car and its many offshoots are personalized to present the reader a vivid picture that the car culture is losing its charm.

翻译 汽车和其很多衍生品（SUV 和皮卡）正在失去对美国人精神和财富的控制。

2.

修辞 contrast

分析 The contrast highlights the difference between young Americans' ideas of cars in the past and at present, to prove that cars are losing their control over the young generation.

翻译 曾经，获得驾照——通常是在 16 或 17 岁时——是一种成熟的仪式。你不再需要父母开车接送。这是踏上成年生活的重要一步。然而，这个标志性事件看起来不再那么重要。

3.

修辞 personification

分析 The car culture is personalized to vividly describe the phenomenon that it does not have much influence on American's mind.

翻译 汽车文化不再如从前一样能够控制美国人的意识。

4.

修辞 metaphor

分析 Prisoners are those who are confined so as to lose their freedom. Therefore, the comparison of "we" to "prisoners" suggests that we are confined by the past so that we may not be free from the car culture so easily.

翻译 我们确实知道的是，我们在很大程度上是过去的囚徒。

V. Language and Style

5.1 Language Analysis

1.

语法标签 分词，宾语从句，并列句

翻　　译 一份来自高速公路损失数据研究所的报道引用研究显示，从 1983 到 2010 年，16 岁的持证驾驶者的占比从 46% 下降到 28%；同一期间，17 岁的持证驾驶者的占比从 69% 下降到 46%。

2.

语法标签 定语从句

翻　　译 据说他们更喜欢自己在城市中能走路、骑自行车、搭乘公车到达商店、餐厅和上班的地方。

3.

语法标签 状语从句

翻　　译 当经济学家在收入、雇佣状态和一些人口因素（婚姻、孩子、教育程度、种族）等方面调整了不同年龄段的购买行为后，他们并没有发现有差异。

4.

语法标签 状语从句，破折号

翻　　译 今天的千禧一代可能会做出不同的选择，虽然这是他们面临的困境——即债务增多、收入缩减——的结果，而非原因。

5.2 Style and Tone

1. studies and reports
2. you
3. we
4. possible extinction of the car culture
5. evidence

VI. Exercises

6.1 Vocabulary

1. D　2. C　3.E　4. A　5. F　6. B

6.2 Text comprehension

1. As indicated in line 1-9, cars have changed America's geography, redefined how we work and play, expanded the heavy industry and became the quintessential symbol of American mobility, status and independence.
2. As revealed in line 15-20, getting a car was a rite of passage to young people, which means that they liberated from dependence on the parental chauffeur.
3. According to line 40-43, young Americans are now so engaged in the Internet that they are unwilling to go out, so it is natural that they do not use cars so much.
4. As suggested in line 57-61, car sales depend on economic factors, rather than permanent shifts in tastes and preferences, so the major reasons for the decreasing influence of cars on youngsters could be high car costs, less income and increased debts.
5. According to line 62-71, many young Americans may decide that they would prefer living in cities or clustered suburban communities, which means that they do not have to drive a car.

Chapter 2 Passage 4

II. Text Structure

1. Anew Internet is arriving.
2. Business between industry and medicine
3. Privacy issues
4. resources Treed by increased efficiency and reduced waste
5. The new Internet brings benefits, although it will not solve all economic problems.

III. Argument Analysis

1. Similar innovations may break down traditional barriers between industry and medicine.
2. The industrial Internet raises privacy issues.
3. the hypothetical example involving pacemakers and other medical implants or wearable medical sensors.
4. daily news about cyberattacks and proliferation of communications among products and infrastructure grids.
5. two hypothetical examples
6. freed resources
7. boosted exports
8. new occupations

IV. Rhetorical Analysis

1.

修辞 metaphor, personification

分析 Sensors are compared to a galaxy to stress the astronomical number of sensors. The industrial Internet is personalized to vividly describe a world where the old is replaced by the new.

翻译 在信息革命的下一个阶段，得益于无线科技和如繁星一样多的传感器的帮助，工业互联网将通过让机器之间能够对话，来打破旧的体系，制造新的机遇。

2.

修辞 contrast

分析 The contrast between manufacturing in the past and at present underscores the benefit brought by the industrial Internet.

翻译 在老式的制造业中，维护通常是次于安装的目标，而且通常由其他公司进行。制造业或服务业通常创立相关公司或创造相关工作。但是现在诊断和预报科技内嵌在产品中，并通过网络进行交流，这使生产商能持续监控产品，并提前纠正问题。

3.

修辞 allusion

分析 The Tower of Babel is an allusion from Old Testament, Genesis. According to Genesis, the Babylonians wanted to make a name for themselves by building a mighty city and a tower "with its top in the heavens." God disrupted the work by so confusing the language of the workers that they could no longer understand one another. The city and the tower were never completed. With the allusion, the author indicates that people are now making efforts to create a common language so that the industrial Internet would not become a failed project as the Tower of Babel.

翻译 有了联邦政府的支持，这次努力，和其他联合以及商业的努力一样，将有助于避免建造一座高科技的"巴别塔"。

4.

修辞 allusion, metaphor

分析 There is an English idiom, "Every cloud has a silver lining" or "Every dark cloud has a silver lining," which means that there is some benefit from every bad thing that happens. According to the idiom, "the dark clouds" refer to the difficulties confronting the economy while "a silver lining" alludes to the benefits brought by the industrial Internet.

翻译 但至少它能给经济正面临的阴云带来一线光明。

V. Language and Style

5.1 Language Analysis

1.

语法标签 同位语，引号，定语从句

翻　　译 GE 公司引入现在已经广泛流传的术语"工业互联网"，专门指正在兴起的物联网的分支，其中包括生产性经济的生产、运输和其他部分。

2.

语法标签 定语从句，并列句，插入语，引号

翻　　译 三大飞机引擎制造商，GE、普惠和劳斯莱斯提供一种名为"按小时提供能源"的模式。根据该模式，制造商们不售卖引擎，而是保留引擎的拥有权，把它们租给航空公司，从而可以给引擎提供终身服务。

3.

语法标签 形式宾语

翻　　译 产品和基础网络之间沟通的激增将使得确保网络安全、使其不受严重损害或攻击变得更必要。

4.

语法标签 状语从句，定语从句

翻　　译 正如早期的互联网创造了全新的产业，例如在线销售和社交媒体咨询，我们今天不能想象的行业也肯定随着机器可以相互沟通而涌现。

5.2 Style and Tone

1. beginning
2. evidence or explanation
3. the advent of the industrial Internet

VI. Exercises

6.1 Vocabulary

1. C 2. E 3.A 4. F 5. D 6. B

6.2 Text Comprehension

1. According to line 9-17, the industrial Internet includes hardware and military drones.
2. As indicated in line 10-29, the new Internet would permit manufacturers to continuously monitor products and correct problems in advance.
3. As line 30-37 states, the aircraft engine manufacturers only sold machines before the industrial Internet is introduced.
4. According to line 57-63, the government could track the public's movements by continuously monitoring their appliances, which is what people would worry about.
5. Line 64-73 implies in its first sentence that robots would receive "great numbers of jobs."

Chapter 2 Passage 5

II. Text Structure

1. Christopher Columbus
2. Indios
3. European and American discovery
4. the Pilgrims in Massachusetts
5. the Pilgrims
6. Wampanoag
7. the Iroquois
8. the Miami Indians
9. the Cherokees
10. end of Indian freedom

III. Argument Analysis

Claim 1

1. Thesis Statement:

   Those Indian tribes that responded to the incursion of whites on their lands with hostility and counter-aggression kept their freedom longer than those that struggled against the whites reluctantly, if at all.

2. Evidence:

   (1) Freedom of tribes resistant to whites

   - Sioux—Began attacking whites during Civil War; battled Army in Powder River country; won Red Cloud's War; defeated Custer; not finally defeated until end of 1890.
   - Apaches—In 1861, Cochise responds to U.S. threat with attack; Apaches evade attempts to put tribe on reservations; Cochise gets desired land for Chiricahua reservation in 1872; Geronimo and other Apaches repeatedly evade hostile whites, leave reservations; guerilla war begun in 1861 only ends in 1886.
   - Cheyennes—Cheyennes successfully resist Army's 1865 invasion of Powder River country; Northern Cheyennes win Red Cloud's War in 1868; Cheyennes join with Sioux, other tribes to defeat Custer in 1876; rebellion at Fort Robinson in 1879; Cheyennes finally subdued in 1880.
   - Navahos—Manuelito launches surprise attack on Fort Defiance in 1860; Navahos refuse to be sent to Bosque Redondo reservation; 1868 treaty wins tribe right to stay off Bosque Redondo and return to homeland.

   (2) Quick subjugation of tribes offering feeble resistance to whites

   - Poncas—Tribe ordered to leave territory in 1877; journeys to Quapaw reservation; Standing Bear's legal efforts ineffectual; in 1879, tribe split in two, with most Poncas moved to Indian Territory.
   - Nez Percés—Tribe signs 1863 treaty giving away most territory; 1877 order for Nez Percés

to leave Wallowa Valley prompts tribe to attempt flight to Canada; tribe caught by Army in late September; Nez Percés sent to Fort Leavenworth, then Lapwai reservation, then Colville reservation.

- Modocs—Captain Jack agrees to treaty removing tribe to Klamath reservation; after skirmish in 1872, tribe retreats to Lava Beds; Captain Jack reluctantly agrees to kill Canby; betrayal of Captain Jack by Hooker Jim ensures tribe's downfall in 1873; tribe sent first to Indian Territory, then to Oregon reservation.
- Utes—1868 treaty reduces size of tribes' territory; in 1873 treaty, tribe sells off mineral-rich land and accepts salary for Ouray; in 1878, agent Meeker arrives and begins pushing for Utes to become agrarian tribe; in 1879, anti-Ute outcry arises; Meeker sends soldiers to subdue tribe; in 1880, nearly all Utes removed to reservation on marginal Utah land.
- Ghost Dance/Wounded Knee Massacre—Sioux adopt Ghost Dance faith in 1890 and cease resisting whites due to prophecy of Indians' return; Sitting Bull killed in December; Minneconjou and Hunkpapa Sioux massacred at Wounded Knee at year's end.

Conclusion:

The Indian tribes that fought against the settlers and the United States government were able to retain their freedom and ways of life longer than the tribes who acquiesced to white demands, or cooperated with the U.S. government.

Claim 2

1. Thesis Statement:

Ordinary white citizens were more responsible for the Indians' defeat than the U.S. government. Without the actions of those citizens, the Army would not have been prompted to make war against the Indians, and the government would not have put the tribes on reservations or made the treaties that pushed them off their land.

(1) Several tribes whose surrender to U.S. began with private white citizens leading invasions against Indians' land and property.

- Santee Sioux—Over 150,000 whites settle on Santee land in 1850s; traders deny Santee food supplies.
- Cheyennes and Arapahos—Pike's Peak gold rush brings thousands of miners to Colorado; settlers come by droves into Platte Valley land held by Southern Cheyennes and Arapahos.
- Apaches—Settlers, miners, freighters invade Apache land; dispute over alleged theft of cattle and boy begins conflict with U.S.
- Modocs—Settlers seize Modoc land in 1850s and 60s; settlers then push for treaty consigning Modocs to Klamath reservation.
- Kiowas and Sioux—White hunters kill off buffalo herds; settlement of Texas plains.
- Oglala Sioux—Miners come into Black Hills; outrage over Custer's defeat prompts push to move Sioux out of Hills.

- Nez Percés—Settlers move into tribes' Wallowa Valley; miners and stockmen steal tribes' horses and cattle; tribe told to move to Lapwai reservation to open up Valley for settlement.
- Utes—Gold rush brings miners into Utes' territory; Colorado citizens push for diminishment of Ute territory; growth of "The Utes Must Go!" slogan creates general clamor to move Utes out of Colorado.

(2) Anti-Indian initiatives supported or engendered by eastern popular sentiment.

- Public pressure on Donehogawa from William Welsh and others leads to his resignation from Commissioner post.
- In wake of Custer's defeat, push from "white men in the East" (p.297) for western Indians to be punished sparks retribution against reservation Indians.
- Support for general doctrine of Manifest Destiny provides ideology to justify subjugation of western Indians.

2. Conclusion:

Western citizens, including settlers, miners, and hunters, give impetus for Army to embark on anti-Indian expeditions and pressure government to remove tribes to reservations. Easterners provide necessary backing and justification for anti-Indian measures taken by U.S. government.

IV. Rhetorical Analysis

1.

修辞 irony

分析 讽刺用在最后一句话 "he apparently decided that he was more English than Indian"，在联姻之后，明显得确定了他与英国人更亲近，而不是印第安人。

翻译 为了在詹姆士镇可以长久安稳，他们（英国人）把金冠戴到了 Wahunsonacook 的头上，授予他波瓦坦国王，并劝他让印第安人为白人提供食物。Wahunsonacook 在反叛民众和英国人之间摇摆不定，但当 John Rolfe 娶了他的女儿 Pocahontas 之后，他明确决定了与英国人更亲近，而不是印第安人。

2.

修辞 parallelism

分析 作者使用平行结构，排比句式列举印第安人为定居的欧洲人提供的帮助，体现帮助之大。

翻译 他和其他印第安人把定居的普利茅斯的定居者看作是无助的孩子们；与他们分享部落存储的玉米，教他们到什么地方怎么抓鱼，帮他们度过了第一个冬天。当春天到来时，他们给白人一些玉米种子，教他们怎么种植和培植玉米。

3.

修辞 imagery

分析 作者通过斧头、倒塌的树以及这些事物发出的声音在整个大陆上回荡，描绘了一幅美洲大陆被外来者破环的整体景象。

翻译 斧头砍伐声和树的倒塌声回荡在这片被白人称为“新英格兰”的临海大陆上。

4.

修辞 irony

分析 这句话讽刺在，这是一个割地协议，作者却使用“to humor”“strange”和“ceremony”。

翻译 然而，他迁就这些陌生人的方式很奇怪，他举行一场土地转移仪式，并在纸上留下了自己的印记。

V. Language Analysis

1.

语法标签 时间状语从句，平行结构

分　析 As 做时间状语从句，理解为“当……时”，从句中三个介词形成并列结构，moved 动词后三个介词“through, down, and then up”，描述了欧洲殖民者步步为营侵入到印第安人的家乡的过程。

翻　译 随着欧洲殖民者穿过阿利根尼山脉，深入到向西流动的河流到达五大湖（密西西比河），然后占据了大马迪湖（密苏里河），类似于上述（侵占）事件，在两个世纪间反复上演。

2.

语法标签 平行结构

翻　译 荷兰士兵用他们的刺刀刺穿了男人、女人和孩子们，砍碎他们的身体，然后放火烧平了整个村庄。

3.

语法标签 非谓语动词；meant to do 作后置定语，对 war 进行定语修饰。

翻　译 1675 年，在殖民者一系列蛮横的行为之后，飞利浦国王带领着他的联合军参加了一场从灭亡中拯救部落的战争。

4.

语法标签 非谓语作状语

翻　译 在新大陆各部落之间的交流缓慢，欧洲人粗野的新闻很少能赶上新一轮征服者和定居者的快速涌入。

VI. Exercises

6.1 Vocabulary

1. tractable	2. decorous	3. scour	4. loot	5. levied tribute
6. retaliated	7. ceding	8. enactment	9. breaches	10. lofty

6.2 Text Comprehension

1. The Taino, in San Salvador.
2. Samoset, Massasoit, Squanto, and Hobomah volunteered to aid the Pilgrims because they knew some English.
3. King Philip of Pokanoket.
4. The Indians called Andrew Jackson "Sharp Knife."
5. The Sioux.

Passage 1

II. Text Structure

1. honeybees foraging earlier
2. colony collapse (within weeks)
3. Clint Perry
4. Andrew Barron
5. precocious
6. experimental
7. normal
8. foraging
9. age demographics
10. 14
11. less
12. mortality
13. negative
14. destroy
15. Randy Oliver
16. fits
17. Dennis van Engelsdorp
18. field tested
19. diagnose/identify
20. at risk of collapse

III. Argument Analysis

Supporting detail 1:

"Since the younger bees are not as good at it, they are going to die sooner, and they're going to not be bringing back as much food, thereby causing more younger bees to go out, and more younger bees to not do as well, and that will cause continuous feedback that will destroy the colony in a short time," said Perry.

Supporting detail 2:

"What you see is what people report in a colony collapse situation," said Barron. "The colony looks like it's doing OK. It looks like it's doing what normal colonies do — it's got high feed, it's got foragers, it's got brood, but you come back about two weeks later and you've got an empty box."

Supporting detail 3:

California beekeeper Randy Oliver, who was not involved in the study, said the model fits the evidence he has documented.

"What we observe in the field is the sign of a poor bee-to-brood ratio, an indicator that adult bees are dying more rapidly than the colony can replace them," Oliver said. "Sudden collapse may soon follow."

Counterclaim 4:

University of Maryland entomologist Dennis van Engelsdorp cautioned that the modeled scenarios will have to be field tested.

"It would be great to see similar work when colonies with normal age distributions are manipulated by removing one age cohort and then seeing how the model holds up," he said.

V. Language and Style

5.1 Language Focus

1. C　2. D　3. A　4. A　5. A
6. D　7. A　8. D　9.D　10. B

5.2 Language Analysis

1.

语法标签　宾语从句，分词后置定语

分　　析　主语：the study；谓语：showed

宾语从句：that too many young bees can cause a tipping point in the tightly regulated social dynamics of a hive

分词后置定语：published online Monday in the journal Proceedings of the National Academy of Sciences

分词后置定语：leaving the hive

分词状语：leading to colony collapse within weeks

翻　　译　这项研究发表在美国国家科学院学报的周一网报上，它表明，太多的年轻蜜蜂离开蜂巢，会导致一个原本紧密规范运转的蜂巢突然达到引爆点，导致在几周内蜂群崩溃。

2.

语法标签　插入语

分　　析　主语：the model；谓语：showed

宾语从句：if mortality roughly doubled, the colony would be locked in a negative feedback loop of more young bees

分词后置定语：foraging at younger ages

分词状语：leading to less stored food and fewer brood—baby bees

翻　　译　但是，该模型显示，如果死亡率大约增加了一倍，该蜂群将会陷入封闭的恶性循环中，更多的年轻蜜蜂提早觅食，导致存储的食物更少以及雏蜜也就是小蜜蜂更少。

3.

语法标签　名词并列

分　　析　主语：studies；谓语：have linked... to...

名词并列：Varroa destructor mites, the gut parasite Nosema, and certain pesticides and agricultural chemicals

分词后置定语：leaving the hive much earlier

翻　　译　有研究表明，在迪斯瓦螨螨、肠道寄生虫、某些杀虫剂和农用化学品的压力下，会导致早熟觅食——也就是说蜜蜂离开蜂巢更早。

4.

语法标签　定语从句，介词短语并列

分　析 主语：the priority；谓语：is；表语：finding ways

定语从句：that we can identify colonies at risk of failure as early as possible so you can intervene and do whatever you need to do to support them and to help heal themselves

介词短语并列：to support them and to help heal themselves

翻　译 “最首要的是找到办法可以尽早识别哪些蜂群已面临危险，这样你就可以干预和做任何你需要做的来帮助支持它们，并帮助它们摆脱困境。”

5.

语法标签 宾语从句，倒装，句子并列，动词并列

分　析 主语：the data；谓语：showed

宾语从句并列句：bees began going on exploratory flights, and they spent less time outside, completed fewer flights and were less likely to survive their first foray

动词并列：spent less time outside, completed fewer flights and were less likely to survive their first foray

翻　译 数据显示：没有任何社会禁忌，高压蜂巢里的小蜜蜂成长不到 14 天就开始了觅食的探索之旅，而且它们无法在外待更长时间，完成趟数少，最终极有可能在它们第一次觅食期间就丧命。

6.

语法标签 同位语，同位语从句

分　析 主语：what we observe in the field；谓语：is

表语：the sign of a poor bee-to-brood ratio；同位语：an indicator

同位语从句：that adult bees are dying more rapidly than the colony can replace them

翻　译 “我们在现场观察到了蜜蜂育雏率的低比例的征兆，表明了成年蜜蜂的死亡速度比更新换代还快，”奥利弗说。

7.

语法标签 形式主语，分词并列

分　析 主语：to see similar work；谓语：would be；表语：great

时间状语从句：when colonies with normal age distributions are manipulated by removing one age cohort and then seeing how the model holds up

分词并列：removing one age cohort and then seeing how the model holds up

翻　译 “很高兴能看到更多类似的研究工作：正常年龄分布的蜂群被人为操纵去掉一个年龄组，然后看看该模型如何成立，”他说。

VI. Exercises

6.1 Vocabulary

1. C　　2. E　　3. B　　4. G　　5. A　　6. F　　7. D

8. foray
9. forage
10. jeopardized
11. buffer
12. manipulate
13. precocious
14. collaborated

6.2 Text Comprehension

1. How bees make decisions and communicate in ways that contribute to a social "superorganism."
2. Miniature radio frequency identification tags.
3. The colony would be locked in a negative feedback loop of more young bees foraging at younger ages, leading to less stored food and fewer brood—baby bees.
4. The observation in the field was the sign of a poor bee-to-brood ratio, which indicated that adult bees were dying more rapidly than the colony could replace them, leading to sudden collapse in a short time.

Chapter 3 Passage 2

II. Text Structure

1. peatlands influence the climate
2. accumulation of carbon
3. easy to catch fire
4. bogs stop recovering after fire

III. Argument Analysis

1.

To provide examples to support the idea in paragraph 12—they take thousands of years to develop. And in five minutes, a wildfire can blow through that area and release five to six hundred years of peat accumulation and change it forever.

2.

First, peat is generally resistant to burning, because sphagnum moss, which is dominant in a healthy bog, holds a lot of water.

Warming, however, alters the system. Drier peat allows more oxygen to get to the roots of trees and other vegetation. This causes them to grow bigger, which means they use more water, further drying the peat.

As trees grow, they also provide more shade, which favors the growth of other mosses that, because they hold less moisture than sphagnum, are less fire resistant.

When the bog does catch fire, it may be more severe, with the combustion spreading deeper into the peat.

Second, normally a bog recovers slowly after a wildfire, with certain mosses and other vegetation taking over in stages until sphagnum mosses dominate.

But an intense fire, or a combination of other factors, can delay or even halt recovery.

V. Language and Style

5.1 Language Analysis

语法标签 定语从句，原因状语从句

分　析 that are less fire resistant 为修饰 mosses 的定语从句。中间插入了 because they hold less moisture than sphagnum 这个原因状语从句。该句子的阅读重点为：As trees grow, they also provide more shade, which favors the growth of other mosses that, because they hold less moisture than sphagnum, are less fire resistant.

翻　译 随着树木的生长，更多阳光被挡住了，这有利于其他苔藓的生长。而这些苔藓比起泥炭藓来说含有的水分较少，所以也更易燃。

5.2 Style and Tone

C

VI. Exercises

6.1 Vocabulary

1. brink　2. smolders　3. teem　4. Resilient　5. susceptible

6.2 Text comprehension

1. Because in peat bogs, it accumulates carbon from sphagnum and moss for a very long time. So, the burning will release most part of the carbon as carbon dioxide into the atmosphere.
2. No. In the last paragraph, "Like, if this was to burn again? Who knows, really, what's going to happen", the author suggests that they have no idea about the solution.

Chapter 3 Passage 3

II. Text Structure

1. the ranking system 2. plan 3. problem 4. problem 5. enormous
6. starting 7. detailing plans 8. manufactures 9. debate

III. Argument Analysis

1. A ranking system; from the title and /or paragraph 1
2. The reagents will need to have separate ranking systems for different kinds of experiments. The author uses an example to support his claim.
3. The debate about the calculation of the scores and the disclosure of the details will be fierce.

IV. Language Analysis

1.

语法标签 条件状语从句，定语从句

分　析 本句为 If 引导的条件状语从句，理解为“如果…”；that 引导的定语从句修饰 antibody，句子主干为“an antibody can be ineffective if...”

翻　译 例如，一个能够精确探测到破碎细胞中蛋白质的抗体，却不能有效地探测完整组织中同样的蛋白质。

2.

语法标签 主语从句

分　析 本句的主语是一个句子，为主语从句，句子主语为“where researchers would look up the scores and the data behind them”。

翻　译 研究者们应该到哪里去查阅他们背后的分数和数据依然不明确，这些数据又该如何审查同样也不明确。

3.

语法标签 宾语从句，定语从句

分　析 本句第一个 that 引导宾语从句做 hopes 的宾语；第二个 that 引导定语从句修饰 antibodies。句子主干为“Anita Bandrowski hopes that... that...”

翻　译 加利福尼亚圣地亚哥大学的信息科学家 Anita Bandrowski 希望生产者们不仅要给抗体记分，而且还要提供因表现不佳而失去连续性的抗体的目录。

4.

语法标签 定语从句，分词作后置定语

分　　析 本句中 who 引导定语从句修饰 researchers; 现在分词 proposing 作定语修饰 paper，句子主干为 “Bandrowski is one of a group of researchers who...”

翻　　译 Bandrowski 是研究组成员，研究组在会议之前发表了一篇论文，文中提出了五个有助于辨认抗体的大概策略。

V. Exercises

5.1 Vocabulary

1. E	2. A	3. D	4. C	5. B
6. D	7. B	8. A	9. C	10. B

5.2 Text Comprehension

1. A	2. D	3.D	4. B	5. A

Passage 4

II. Text Structure

1. The questioning of term "food desert" and efficacy of the interventions
2. food desert
3. how to approach so-called food desert
4. the approach to food desert need to be further studied

III. Argument Analysis

1. To support the ideas that the term "food desert" has been debated among scholars.
2. To support the ideas "such a basic definition renders interventions to be one-dimensional and less effective."

V. Language and Style

5.1 Language Analysis

语法标签 定语从句

分　析 As Sadler explains, it's the simplicity of the definition that makes it appealing to some and can lead to interventions that are straight forward, like placing a grocery store in an area that is deemed a food desert.

翻　译 正如 Sadler 所解释的那样，它是概念的简化形式，不仅吸引了部分人群，也能使问题的解决措施直截了当，比如在一个被认为是“食品沙漠”的社区建立一个杂货零售店。

5.2 Style and Tone

E

VI. Exercises

6.1 Vocabulary

1. attune　2. embrace　3. render　4. efficacy　5. insurgency

6.2 Text Comprehension

1. F　2. F　3.T　4. F　5. F　6. F

Passage 5

I. Warm Up

1.3 Reading Skills

1.3.1 Skimming

1. The woman suffers from locked-in syndrome, which paralyzes her and makes her unable to breathe or communicate on her own.
2. The device enables the woman to select letters on a computer screen using her mind alone and helps her spell out words to communicate her thoughts.

II. Text Structure

Paragraph 1 & 2

The author introduces a wireless device that helps a paralyzed woman with locked-in syndrome to communicate. He gives a detailed description to the woman's situation in the second paragraph.

Paragraph 3

The device enables the woman to select letters on a computer screen, spelling out words at a rate of one letter every 56 seconds to share her thoughts.

Paragraph 4

The previous devices helped the woman to communicate using a system that uses an infrared camera to track her eye movements. Such devices are awkward to set up and used by someone who cannot move, and they do not function well in many situations, such as in bright sunlight.

Paragraph 5

A wire penetrating the skin carries risk of infection. But the new device is advanced because it uses wireless communication with the computer.

Paragraph 7

People oppose implantation as a means to help patients with the Locked-in Syndrome and suggest that recording brain wave should be adopted as an alternative.

Paragraph 8

The author states that "Recording brain waves through the skull, however, currently lacks the sensitivity needed to tap into the neural circuits that control fine voluntary movements."

III. Argument Analysis

Paragraph 1 & 2

The author builds imagery of the research subject—a 59-year-old woman suffering from locked-in syndrome, who is unable to breathe, move or speak on her own.

Meanwhile, the author introduces the new "wireless device" which has enabled the woman to communicate her thoughts from the comfort of her home by recording brain waves.

Paragraph 3

The author mainly rely on data to further describe the new device, which enables the woman to select letter on computer screen and spell one letter every 56 seconds to share her thoughts.

Paragraph 4 & 5

The author presents a specific example that a system which uses an infrared camera to track the eye movements was adopted to help the woman to communicate. But the author claims that the device is awkward because it is difficult to set up and use for someone who cannot move, and it does not function well in many situations, such as in bright sunlight. Other examples that couple neural activity, for example, implantation of electrodes into brains, are also discussed in Paragraph 5.

Paragraph 6

The author discusses concerns regarding to new device that surgically implanting electrodes into the brain carries inherent risks. He quotes expert that "anytime there is a wire penetrating the skin there is risk of infection." However, the quotation from the experts helps ease such concerns, saying that "this new study is an advance because the implant uses wireless communication with the computer. It is really important to bring this capability home, and they have done that."

Paragraph 7

The author discusses objection to the new device, saying that "the technology is not with controversy." Expert opinions are cited that "some experts believe that only noninvasive methods should be used to help people with locked-in syndrome to communicate" and "implantation like the one reported here may carry an unknown risk for advanced ALS patients." To be more specific, recording brain waves from scalp electrodes is introduced as an alternative.

Paragraph 8

First, the author refutes recording brain waves as a practical alternative, claiming it "lacks the sensitivity needed to tap into the neural circuits that control fine voluntary movements." Then, the author borrows expert opinion to further undermine the suggested alternative that "it takes a team of highly specialized technicians to attach the electrodes to the electroencephalography (EEG) cap and operate an EEG recording station", which is beyond the capacities of caregivers. Moreover, expert opinion states that the EEG's inhibitive effects on interaction of patients would prevent it as a feasible solution.

Paragraph 9, 10 & 11

First, the author refutes recording brain waves as a practical alternative, claiming it "lacks the sensitivity needed to tap into the neural circuits that control fine voluntary movements." Then, the author borrows expert opinion to further undermine the suggested alternative that "it takes a team of highly specialized technicians to attach the electrodes to the electroencephalography (EEG) cap and operate an EEG recording station", which is beyond the capacities of caregivers. Moreover, expert opinion states that the EEG's inhibitive effects on interaction of patients would prevent it as a feasible solution.

IV. Language and Style

4.1 Language Analysis

1.

语法标签 分词

分　析 The new wireless device enables her to select letters on a computer screen <u>using</u> her mind alone, <u>spelling</u> out words at a rate of one letter every 56 seconds, to share her thoughts.

翻　译 这个新的无线设备，使 HB 能单独用大脑，就能在电脑屏幕中选出字母，并以 56 秒完成一个字母的速度拼写单词，以表达想法。

2.

语法标签 定语从句，并列句，原因状语从句

分　析 HB' s mind is intact and the part of her brain <u>that</u> controls her bodily movements operates perfectly, <u>but</u> the signals from her brain no longer reach her muscles because the motor neurons <u>that</u> relay them have been damaged by amyotrophic lateral sclerosis (ALS), says neuroscientist Erick Aarnoutse, <u>who</u> designed the new device and was responsible for the technical aspects of the research.

翻　译 HB 的思维无损，并且控制运动的大脑部分也能完好运作，但是大脑信号不能传达至肌肉，因为连接肌肉的运动神经元被ALS所破坏，神经科学家Erick Aarnoutse如是说，这位神经科学家设计出这个新的设施并负责其技术层面的研究。

4.2 Style and Tone

1. Niels Birbaumer　　2. Kennedy　　3. 2　　4. HB

V. Exercises

5.1 Vocabulary

1. B　　2. C　　3.A

5.2 Text Comprehension

1. The new device is an advance because the implant uses wireless communication with the computer.
2. First, surgically implanting electrodes into the brain carries inherent risks of infection. Some experts even believe that only noninvasive methods should be adopted to help people with locked-in syndrome. Moreover, some experts claims that the communication speed brought about by the new device, that is, one to two letters per minutes, may not justify the risks.
3. First, the author refutes that some experts' suggestion that recording brain waves as an alternative to implantation. The author denies that "recording brain waves through the skull" is a practical approach because it "lacks the sensitivity needed to tap into the neutral circuits that control fine voluntary movement". Moreover, he specifies that the EEG requires specialized technicians to operate, which is far beyond the capacities of caretakers. Also, the inhibitive effect on interaction of EGG prevents it as a feasible solution. Then, the author cites expert testimony that "locked-in people can lead meaningful and productive lives if they can communicate", and uses HB as an example who has gained freedom and more independence since the implantation has given her the ability to communicate" to strengthen his view.

Chapter 4 Passage 1

II. Text Structure

1. government / administration
2. prosecute the war (with Germany)
3. wish
4. will
5. approval
6. confidence
7. battle / crisis
8. blood, toil, tears and sweat
9. to wage war
10. victory

III. Argument Analysis

1. I have completed the most important part of this task.
2. The three party leaders... executive office. (line 12-14)
   The three fighting services have been filled. (line 14)

V. Language and Style

5.1 Language Focus

1. C	2. D	3. C	4. B	5. B
6. D	7. A	8. A	9. C	10. D

5.2 Language Analysis

1.

语法标签 转折结构

分　析 结构：The appointment takes a little longer, but...

翻　译 其他一些大臣的任命，虽然通常需要更多一点的时间，但是，我相信再次开会时，我的这项任务将会完成，而且本届政府在各方面都将是完整无缺的。

2.

语法标签 定语从句

分　析 结构：I would say to the House, as I said to those who...

翻　译 正如我曾对参加本届政府的成员所说的那样，我要向下院说："我没什么可以奉献，只有热血、辛劳、眼泪和汗水。"

3.

语法标签 并列结构

分析 结构：It is to wage war, by sea, land and air, with all our might and...

翻译 我要说，我们的政策就是用我们的全部能力，用上帝所给予我们的全部力量，在海上、陆地和空中进行战争，同一个在人类黑暗悲惨的罪恶史上所从未有过的穷凶极恶的暴政进行战争。

VI. Exercises

6.1 Vocabulary

1. E	2. D	3. A	4. C	5. B
6.B	7. A	8. A	9. D	10. A

6.2 Text Comprehension

1. D	2. C	3. A	4. D
5. A	6. D	7. D	8. A

II. Text Structure

1. discrimination 2. Paris 3. America 4. open her mouth
5. "You must get an education. You must go to school, and you must learn to protect yourself. And you must learn to protect yourself with the pen, and not the gun." and "But I want to take credit for telling you how to do the same thing, and when you scream, friends, I know you will be heard. And you will be heard now."

III. Text Analysis

1. America: When I left St. Louis a long time ago, the conductor directed me to the last car.
   Paris: I could go into any restaurant I wanted to, and I could drink water anyplace I wanted to, and I didn' t have to go to a colored toilet either.
2. But on that great big beautiful ship, I had a bad experience. A very important star was to sit with me for dinner, and at the last moment I discovered she didn' t want to eat with a colored woman. I can tell you it was some blow.
3. Friends and brothers and sisters, that is how it went. And when I screamed loud enough, they started to open that door just a little bit, and we all started to be able to squeeze through it. Not just the colored people, but the others as well, the other minorities too, the Orientals, and the Mexicans, and the Indians, both those here in the United States and those from India.
4. You must get an education. You must go to school, and you must learn to protect yourself. And you must learn to protect yourself with the pen, and not the gun. Then you can answer them, and I can tell you—and I don't want to sound corny—but friends, the pen really is mightier than the sword.

IV. Rhetorical Analysis

1.

修辞 metaphor

分析 此处使用了比喻的修辞手法，歧视之于少数人群就像紧闭的门之于想进门的人，歧视就像关紧门一样，当她呼喊的声音足够大时门就打开了一点。演讲者以这种方式来传达她的想法和对群众的鼓励，其信息更容易被听众理解和接受。

翻译 当我大声呼吁时，他们开始把那扇门打开了一点，我们都能够挤过去。不仅是黑人，其他少数群体、东方人、墨西哥人、印度人、印度安人等其他人也都可以进去。

2.

修辞 parallelism

分析 演讲者使用排比来加强其建议的重要性，使之更具有表达力和感染力。

翻译 你必须要获得教育，你必须要去学校，你必须要学会去保护自己。你必须要学会用笔来保护自己，而不是枪。

3.

修辞 parallelism

分析 演讲者使用排比来加强其建议的重要性，使之更具有表达力和感染力。

翻译 这样你才能坚持下去，这样你才能做到我做过的事情。

4.

修辞 parallelism

分析 演讲者使用排比来加强其建议的重要性，使之更具有表达力和感染力。

翻译 现在，我不会站在你们面前居功于今天发生的一切，我不能那么做。但是我很荣幸地告诉你们如何去做同样的事情。当你们呼喊出来，朋友们，我知道你们会被听到的。

V. Language and Style

5.1 Language Focus

1. A	2. D	3. C	4. D	5. A
6. B	7. C	8. B	9. B	10. D

5.2 Language Analysis

1.

语法标签 for

分析 Coordinating conjunction "for" 连接两个句子，引出原因。

翻译 让这片土地变得安全，这样他们（孩子们）不必再躲避，因为我想让你们和你们的孩子们得到我所得到的。

2.

语法标签 强调，宾语从句，状语从句

分析 did 在句中强调动词 open 和 scream；what I was supposed to have and what I was 作 entitled to 和 demand 的宾语从句；when I demand 作 they still would not give it to me 的状语从句。

翻译 所以我大声呼喊，你知道当我呼喊时，当我要求我本应该且有资格获得的东西时，他们仍然不给我。

VI. Exercises

6.1 Vocabulary

1. blow 2. was entitled to 3. smear 4. communist 5. hounded
6. squeeze 7. take credit for 8. fashion 9. corny 10. mightier

6.2 Text Comprehension

1.

When she was in New York, she was not allowed to check into the good hotels or eat in certain restaurants because she was colored.

Evidence in the speech:

And when I got to New York way back then, I had other blows—when they would not let me check into the good hotels because I was colored, or eat in certain restaurants.

You know, friends that I do not lie to you when I tell you I have walked into the palaces of kings and queens and into the houses of presidents. And much more. But I could not walk into a hotel in America and get a cup of coffee, and that made me mad. And when I get mad, you know that I open my big mouth.

2.

It applies as a support for her speech:

Baker mentioned she got an invitation to the White House by the white president to support what she claimed in her speech: when you scream, friends, I know you will be heard. And you will be heard now; you must get an education. You must go to school, and you must learn to protect yourself. And you must learn to protect yourself with the pen, and not the gun. Then you can answer them, and I can tell you—and I don' t want to sound corny—but friends, the pen really is mightier than the sword.

It applies as an encouragement for her audience:

Baker actually got the honor she deserved by crying out loud for what she deserved and by getting education to answer white people with pen. She encouraged them: Someday I want your children out there to have that great honor too. And we know that that time is not someday. We know that that time is now.

3.

She refused to go to the White House.

Evidence in the speech:

Ladies and gentlemen, my friends and family, I have just been handed a little note, as you probably say. It is an invitation to visit the President of the United States in his home, the White House.

I am greatly honored. But I must tell you that a colored woman—or, as you say it here in America, a black woman—is not going there. It is a woman. It is Josephine Baker.

4.

It was an assertion of her independence as an African-American woman.

Chapter 4 Passage 3

II. Text Structure

1. the families of victims
2. the people of Oklahoma City and Oklahoma state
3. all Americans present
4. the American people
5. parents
6. husband and wife
7. your neighbors
8. mourn
9. share
10. thank
11. heal
12. rebuild
13. bring to justice
14. innocent
15. citizens
16. neighbors
17. allow yourselves to be consumed by it
18. be allowed to turn into hate
19. paralyze your own lives
20. search for justice
21. try to pay tribute to your loved ones
22. selfless
23. love
24. caring
25. courage
26. the dark forces
27. violence
28. evil
29. plant a tree
30. a long time
31. begin

III. Argument Analysis

1. The anger you feel is valid, but you must not allow yourselves to be consumed by it. The hurt you feel must not be allowed to turn into hate, but instead into the search for justice. The loss you feel must not paralyze your own lives. Instead, you must try to pay tribute to your loved ones by continuing to do all the things they left undone, thus ensuring they did not die in vain.
2. If ever we needed evidence of that, I could only recall the words of Governor and Mrs. Keating: "If anybody thinks that Americans are mostly mean and selfish, they ought to come to Oklahoma. If anybody thinks Americans have lost the capacity for love and caring and courage, they ought to come to Oklahoma."
3. Yesterday, Hillary and I had the privilege of speaking with some children of other federal employees—children like those who were lost here. And one little girl said something we will never forget. She said, "We should all plant a tree in memory of the children." So this morning before we got on the plane to come here, at the White House, we planted that tree in honor of the children of Oklahoma. It was a dogwood with its wonderful spring flower and its deep, enduring roots.

IV. Rhetorical Analysis

1.

修辞 symploce

分析 The same sentence structure is employed by the two sentences: some children of other federal employees—children like those who were lost here. And one little girl said something we...

翻译 当听到仇恨的言论时，让我们站起来反驳它。当听到暴力的言论时，让我们站起来反驳它。

2.

修辞 parallelism

分析 "... feel is ..." "and you must not..." are repeated

翻译 你们感到愤怒，这合情合理，但请不要因此消沉。你们感到伤害，但请不要把它变成仇恨，而变成寻求正义的力量。你们感到失去，但请不要让它麻痹你们的生活。

3.

修辞 parallelism

分析 "who worked to..."is repeated to introduce to us the victims are people who contributed a lot to our country.

翻译 他们曾帮助老年人和残疾人，他们曾支持我们的农民和军人，他们曾致力于执行法律来保护我们。

4.

修辞 allusion

分析 The sentence comes from Romans 12:21—"Do not be overcome by evil, but overcome evil with good."

翻译 不要被恶所胜，要以善胜恶。

5.

修辞 asyndeton

分析 The usual expression is "as..., as..., and as...". "And"is omitted here.

翻译 我今天来到这里，和希拉里作为父母、作为丈夫和妻子、作为生活中最要好的邻居。

V. Language and Style

5.1 Language Analysis

1.

语法标签 同位语，代词并列

分　析 主语：we；谓语：thank；宾语：all those；同位语：—；代词并列：those...and those..., and many...

翻　译 我们感谢所有那些曾英勇救人和破案的英雄们——那些生活在俄克拉何马的民众和所有在这广阔的土地上居住的人，以及那些从外地赶来此处援助且同大家并肩作战的人们。

2.

语法标签 表语并列，同位语，定语从句并列

分　析 主语：This terrible sin；谓语：took；宾语：the lives；原因状语从句：only because；表语并列：parents & workers & citizens & many；同位语：—；定语从句并列：who worked to help...; who worked to help...; who worked to support...; who worked to enforce

翻　译 这可怕的罪恶行径夺去了很多美国家庭的生命，其中有无辜的孩子们，只是因为他们的父母都想成为优秀的家长、职工；有每日忙碌工作的市民们；还有许多服务工作者——他们曾帮助老人和残疾人，他们曾大力支持我们的农民和军人，他们曾致力于执行我们的法律，保护我们。

5.2 Style and Tone

1. Create a bond with the audience: we, with you, join, share
2. Criticize the bomb: evil, terrible sin, dark forces
3. Urge people to get over the grief: must not
4. Call to action: let us

VI. Exercises

6.1 Vocabulary

1. E	2. D	3. F	4. C
5. A	6. H	7. B	8. G
9. embodies	10. purged	11. pledged	12. enforce
13. prevail	14. mourned	15. admonished	16. paralyzed

6.2 Text Comprehension

1. She hoped the people wouldn't get lost by the overwhelming grief, and urged them to try to pay tribute to your loved ones by continuing to do all the things they left undone.
2. Let us "not be overcome by evil, but overcome evil with good."
3. There is an analogy employed here to compare wounds and grief to a tree, meaning that a long time is needed to heal.
4. They must have capacity for love and caring and courage.

Passage 4

II. Text Structure

1. of sixteen 2. wife and mother 3. uneducated woman 4. solitude

III. Argument Analysis

1. The main claim of each paragraph appears to be similar. The key word "solitude" and its paraphrasing and related words are repeated throughout the passage.
2. No clear evidence or reasoning can be found in this passage. Instead, the speaker mainly employs pathos and figurative languages to support her claims.

IV. Rhetorical Analysis

1.

修辞 metaphor, parallelism

分析 "Captain", "pilot", and "engineer" mean the different roles in a woman's life, while "to watch the wind and waves" and "to read the signs in the firmament" allude to various tasks that women need to perform.

翻译 为了引导自己的航船，我们必须既是船长，又是导航员，又是工程师，带着海图和罗盘，站立在舵手之位，观察风浪，知道何时卷下风帆，读懂苍穹之上一切迹象。

2.

修辞 imagery, simile

分析 This vivid imagery forces gruesome images into the readers' minds.

翻译 在一个人接受完整教育的道路上设置障碍，就像剜掉人的双眼；拒绝承认人的财产权利，就像砍掉人的双手。

3.

修辞 imagery, pathos, metaphor

分析 Again, Stanton applies imagery by sharing the story of the play, "Titus Andronicus," written by William Shakespeare. The quotations here create a bloody picture, which arouses the readers emotionally. The author also implies that the disfranchised women in 19th century share similar situations with the poor daughter in the play: they are deprived of natural rights, yet compelled to fight their own battles.

翻译 莎士比亚的戏剧《泰特斯·安德洛尼克斯》犀利地嘲讽了19世纪女性的地位——"粗鲁的男人们"（该戏剧讲述给我们）"抓住国王的女儿，割掉她的舌头，砍掉她的双手，然后又要她去弄点水来洗她的双手。”多么形象的一幅描述女性地位的画面。

4.

修辞 metaphor, pathos

分析 Women' s being underprivileged is described to provoke emotions of sympathy and pity. Fighting battles is implicitly compared with struggling for life.

翻译 她的天赋人权被夺走，因法律和习俗而处处受挫，却又被迫独自为战，在生命的紧要关头，只能依靠自己保护自己。

5.

修辞 parallelism

分析 The writer uses grammatically similar structures to emphasize the responsibilities of women and the importance of knowledge.

翻译 但是要持家，要在社会中产生好影响，要维持友情和丈夫对自己的感情，要教好小孩，训好仆人，她就必须具有非同一般的常识、智慧、交际手腕，以及对人性的了解。

6.

修辞 hyperbole, pathos

分析 Women's situation in education and social activities is described to provoke emotions of sympathy and pity.

翻译 然而社会却说女性不需要关于世界的知识，不需要公众生活经验所能提供的充足的训练，不需要大学教育所带来的种种好处。但是当女性因为缺少上述一切，其幸福遭到摧毁之时，她只能独自忍受耻辱。软弱无知者的孤独的确可悲可叹，因为这些人在盲目追求生活奖赏中，被碾成齑粉。

7.

修辞 parallelism, pathos

分析 Stanton refers to the common experience in a typical woman's life to stir up emotions of sympathy.

翻译 当青春的欢娱消逝，当小孩长大成人，结婚离家，当生活的匆忙喧嚣接近尾声，当双手无力从事全职劳作，当旧扶手椅和壁炉边成为常留之地，不管是男人还是女人，都必须转而依靠自己。

8.

修辞 contrast, parallelism, alliteration

分析 Stanton uses similar structures “rich and poor”, “intelligent and ignorant”, “wise and foolish”, “virtuous and vicious”, and “man and woman” to emphasize that every people is equal. Both phrases (“intelligent and ignorant”, “virtuous and vicious”) are alliterative because the same first letters (“I” and “V”) occur close together.

翻译 富人与穷人，智者与愚者，善人与恶人，男人与女人，全都一样，每个人都必须完全依靠自己。

9.

修辞 contrast, metaphor

分析 The “fierce storm” is used to imply difficult situations in life.

翻译 要保护女性，使其免遭生活的狂风暴雨，这种说法是十足的嘲弄，因为生活的风暴对女性如同对男性一样，从四面八方袭击她们，且带来更为致命的后果，因为男性受过训练，知道如何保护自己、如何去抗争、如何去征服，而女性没有。

10.

修辞 comparison, metaphor

分析 Stanton uses several comparisons to imply the inaccessibility, profundity and secrecy of human's solitude.

翻译 有一种孤独是我们每个人随身带有的，它比冰冷的山峦更加不可企及，比午夜的海洋更加深不可测，这就是自我之孤独。我们称为自我的内心世界，不管是凡人还是天使都看不穿、摸不透，它比土地神的洞穴更隐秘，比祭司的神殿内室更隐秘，比依洛西斯城的秘密仪式更隐秘，因为唯有全知的上帝才能进入。

11.

修辞 rhetorical question, parallelism

分析 This rhetorical question is self-evident and used for an impressive persuasive device. The speaker does not expect a real answer.

翻译 试问有谁能够，又有谁敢于将另一人的权利、义务与责任全部承担于己身?

V. Language and Style

5.1 Language Analysis

1.

语法标签 平行结构，定语从句

分　析 The strongest reason why we ask for woman a voice in the government under which she lives; in the religion she is asked to believe; equality in social life, where she is the chief factor; a place in the trades and professions, where she may earn her bread, is because of her birthright to self-sovereignty; because, as an individual, she must rely on herself.

翻　译 我们要求女性在自己的政府中有发言权，在让她们信仰的宗教中有发言权，在她们充当重要角色的社会生活中享受平等待遇，在她们谋生的各行各业中要占有一席之地；之所以这样要求，最大的理由是她们与生俱来的自主权；因为作为一个独立个体，她必须依靠自己。

2.

语法标签 平行结构

分　析 To deny political equality is to rob the ostracized of all self-respect; of credit in the market place; of recompense in the world of work; of a voice in those who make and administer the law; a choice in the jury before whom they are tried, and in the judge who decides their punishment.

翻　译 拒绝接受政治平等相当于夺走被排挤人群的所有自尊，夺走他们在市场中的信用，夺走他们在职场中的报酬，夺走他们在选择立法者和司法者上的发言权，夺走他们选择自己陪审团的自由，夺走他们选择决定自己刑罚的法官的自由。

3.

语法标签 平行结构，时间状语从句

分　析 In age, when the pleasures of youth are passed, children grown up, married and gone, the hurry and bustle of life in a measure over, when the hands are weary of active service, when the old armchair and the fireside are the chosen resorts, then men and women alike must fall back on their own resources.

翻　译 当青春的欢娱消逝，当小孩长大成人，结婚离家，当生活的匆忙喧嚣接近尾声，当双手无力从事全职劳作，当旧扶手椅和火炉边成为常留之地，不管是男人还是女人，都必须转而依靠自己。

4.

语法标签 平行结构

分　析 If from a lifelong participation in public affairs a woman feels responsible for the laws regulating our system of education, the discipline of our jails and prisons, the sanitary condition of our private homes, public buildings, and thoroughfares, an interest in commerce, finance, our foreign relations, in any or all these questions, her solitude will at least be respectable, and she will not be driven to gossip or scandal for entertainment.

翻　译 如果一位女性通过终身参与公共事业，感到对规定我们教育制度的法律负有责任，对我们的看守所和监狱的纪律负有责任，对私人住宅、公共建筑和公共道路的卫生条件负有责任，对商业、财政、外交关系中的个别问题或所有问题有兴趣，那么，她的孤独至少是令人尊敬的，而她自己也不至于以搬弄是非，传播丑闻为乐。

5.2 Style and Tone

1.

These four periods epitomize the whole life of a typical woman in that era. She also appeals to the emotion of women through sharing predicament in different stages, from youth to age, of an exemplary woman living in the same era.

2.

...when the pleasures of youth are passed, children grown up, married and gone, the hurry and bustle of life in a measure over, when the hands are weary of active service, when the old armchair and the fireside are the chosen resorts... (line 70-73)

...there is a solitude, which each and every one of us has always carried with him more inaccessible than the ice-cold mountains, more profound than the midnight sea; the solitude of self. (line 110-113)

It is more hidden than the caves of the gnome; the sacred adytum of the oracle; the hidden chamber of Eleusinian mystery, for to it only omniscience is permitted to enter. (line 114-116)

3.

To guide our own craft, we must be captain, pilot, engineer; with chart and compass to stand at the wheel; to watch the wind and waves and know when to take in the sail, and to read the signs in the firmament over all. (line 18-21)

The talk of sheltering woman from the fierce storms of life is the sheerest mockery, for they beat on her from every point of the compass, just as they do on man... (line 101-103)

4.

...then men and women alike must fall back on their own resources. (line 73-74)

...that the responsibilities of life rest equally on man and woman, that their destiny is the same...(line 99-100)...each soul must depend wholly on itself. (line 108)

VI. Exercises

6.1 Vocabulary

1. wreck	2. faculty	3. lean	4. solitude
5. integrity	6. superstition	7. tempt	8. grind
9. G	10. E	11. A	12. F
13. D	14. B	15. H	16. C
17. A	18. D	19. D	

6.2 Text Comprehension

1. D	2. D	3. B	4. B	5. A

6.

"The voyage" in this passage is used to imply people's whole life.

Other words and images related to the sea include:

Navigation, craft, captain, pilot, engineer, chart, compass, wheel—control over life; things that help to depend on oneself (education, knowledge, interests in public affairs, etc.)

Wind, waves, fierce storm—difficult situations in life

7.

They all show some common experience that can be shared with women in that era, which helps to provoke empathy and pity. The author uses pathos here to reinforce her claim.

Passage 5

II. Text Structure

1. Elucidate
2. principles
3. constitution
4. pernicious
5. standing army
6. baneful aristocracy
7. concession
8. (evidently) absurd
9. union
10. improper delegation
11. opposition
12. best

III. Argument Analysis

1.

The first sentences of paragraph 2, 3, 4, and 6.

They all include some key words or phrases that have negative meanings, such as pernicious tendency, charge, accusation, annihilate, improper delegation.

2.

The author's own claims often appear at the end of each paragraph. We can find them by looking for the structures used to express personal opinions. (The consequence is too obvious to require any further delineation..., for my part..., from this view..., I will venture to predict that..., I am bold to assert that...)

3.

Refutation through evidence / logic

evidence: "Nor is it a novelty... the Ohio" (line 16-19) "But I will confess... reproach" (line 41-46)

reasoning: "The president... supplied" (line 65-68) "The Senate... no Senate" (line 69-71) "The House... extince" (line 71-77)

IV. Rhetorical Analysis

1.

修辞 parallelism

分析 Repetition occurs in similar structured clauses "Whatever may be the provocation", "however important the object in view", and "however necessary dispatch and secrecy may be" to emphasize the importance of national defense.

翻译 不管何种挑衅，不管目标何等重要，不管调遣与保密何等必要，然而宣战总是先于备战，敌人也总会在你做好攻击准备之前，甚至在加强防御之前，就已得知你的意图。

2.

修辞 refutation

分析 Wilson presents reasoning to undermine the opposing claim that the Federal Senate has "the institution of a baneful aristocracy".

翻译 或许可以说，没有任何别的指控，比预言联邦参议院会有一种有害的贵族制倾向更没道理的了。这个机构兼有两种性质，一个是立法性质，一个是执行性质。就其立法性质而言，没有众议院的共同行动，参议院就无法实现任何目的；就其执行性质而言，没有总统的同意，参议院也无法实现它的目标。受到如此的牵制，我不知道它还能独自制定什么法律。参议院的这种依附性，不可能使它拥有很大的影响或者优越地位。

3.

修辞 jargon

分析 The speaker intends to explicitly convey the hidden meanings of the term "corporation" which need to be accepted and understood in different situations.

翻译 那些对此场合使用"法人"这一术语的人也许没有注意到这个词的范围。按照通常的意义，它确实适用于小型联盟，这类联盟是为了一小部分人的方便自在而设立；但在更大的意义上，这个词包括宾夕法尼亚州政府，现在的邦联，甚至这一规划中的体系（指宪法）不外乎也是一项设立法人的正式法律。（"设立法人"此处指组建政府这一法律实体）

4.

修辞 induction

分析 The speaker reaches a conclusion through reasoning.

翻译 总统由选举人挑选，选举人则以各州议会指示的方式提名；所以若无州议会，则无选举人，总统办公室也无法组成。

5.

修辞 metaphor

分析 Wilson made an implicit comparison between "seeds" and "reformation" that are unrelated but share some common characteristics: they cannot be seen immediately, but some possibilities exist just there.

翻译 如果宪法出现错误，我们应该牢记改良的种子就播撒于宪法自身，国会可以在任何时间以三分之二的通过率来对宪法提出变更和修正。

V. Language and Style

5.1 Language Analysis

1.

语法标签 平行结构，状语从句

分　析 Whatever may be the provocation, however important the object in view, and however necessary dispatch and secrecy may be, still the declaration must precede the preparation, and the enemy will be informed of your intention, not only before you are equipped for an attack, but even before you are fortified for a defense.

翻　译 不管是何种挑衅，不管目标何等重要，不管调遣与保密何等必要，然而宣战总会先于备战，敌人也总会在你做好攻击准备之前，甚至在加强防御之前，就已得知你的意图。

2.

语法标签 宾语从句，“rather...than...”结构

分　析 ...this evidence of mutual concession and accommodation ought rather to command a generous applause, than to excite jealousy and reproach.

翻　译 但我承认，在组建这一机构（指参议院）的过程中，在利益发生冲突时，我们看到了各方都做出让步。当我们意识到组成联邦的各州在法律、商业、习惯、人口和范围方面的差异时，（我们就会感到）这种相互的妥协与包容理应博得慷慨的掌声，而不应激起嫉妒与责难。

3.

语法标签 平行结构，定语从句

分　析 ...when we consider it as the duty of that body to provide for the national safety, to support the dignity of the union, and to discharge the debts contracted upon the collected faith of the States for their common benefit...those upon whom such important obligations are imposed, ought in justice and in policy to possess every means requisite for a faithful performance of their trust.

翻　译 类似地，直接征税的权力也被视为一项对联邦政府的不当授权；但是当我们将这一权力视为联邦政府的一种责任，以求确保国家安全，维护联邦尊严，以及清偿那些基于合众国共同信念、为了合众国共同利益所签订的债务时，我们必须承认，无论在正义上，还是在政治上，那些担负如此重要义务（指纳税）的人们应当拥有所有必要手段，来保证他们的委托（指前文的“确保国家安全，维护联邦尊严，以及清偿……债务”）能被忠实地执行。

4.

语法标签 平行结构，虚拟语气

分　析 I will confess, indeed, that I am not a blind admirer of this plan of government, and that there are some parts of it which, if my wish had prevailed, would certainly have been altered.

翻　译 我承认，我确实不是这个政府的设计方案的盲目崇拜者，我也承认如果我的意愿优先的话，这个方案必然会有一些变更之处。

5.2 Tone and Style

1. ...yet I do not know a nation in the world which has not found it necessary and useful to maintain the appearance of strength...

   Congress certainly possesses...

   But what would be our national situation were it otherwise?

   ...must be subverted···must declare war...

   ...no man ... can deny the necessity of a military force.

2. double negative: ...no man ... can deny the necessity of a military force

rhetorical question: But what would be our national situation were it otherwise?

modal verb: must

adverb: certainly

VI. Exercises

6.1 Vocabulary

1. impost	2. legislature	3. amendment	4. constitution
5. C	6. D	7. G	8. H
9. E	10. B	11. F	12. A
13. B	14. B		

6.2 Text Comprehension

1. B 2. C 3. A 4. C 5. C

6.

The writer often directly or indirectly cited a view of opponents, then refuted it. Therefore, the opposing views can be found in the opening sentence of each body paragraph.

Besides, Wilson made no distortion when reporting the opposing side' s position, so words with negative meaning often appear in the first sentence, including "pernicious", "charge", "accusation", "annihilate", "improper".

7.

The opponents' view is that "The next accusation...is that which represents the Federal constitution, as not only calculated, but designedly framed, to reduce the State governments to mere corporations and eventually to annihilate them."

Wilson explicitly listed the special and general meanings of the term "corporation", and then reasoned that in the general sense, it is impossible to annihilate a "corporation".

Chapter 5 | # Passage 1

II. Text Structure

1. Motives   2. A painful truth   3. Our Strategies   4. Reinforcement

III. Argument Analysis

We have petitioned; we have remonstrated; we have supplicated; we have prostrated ourselves before the throne, and have implored its interposition to arrest the tyrannical hands of the ministry and Parliament. Our petitions have been slighted; our remonstrances have produced additional violence and insult; our supplications have been disregarded; and we have been spurned, with contempt, from the foot of the throne!

IV. Rhetorical Analysis

1.

修辞 allusion

分析 犹大之吻是《圣经》中的故事，象征着背叛、死亡、口蜜腹剑。通常用来形容背叛朋友而又装得十分亲热的叛徒嘴脸，比如可耻的变节和叛变行为。

翻译 不要让自己因为一个亲吻就遭到出卖和背叛。

2.

修辞 metaphor

分析 作者以灯为经验的暗喻，意味着经验可以像灯光一样在黑暗之中指引方向，驱散黑暗和迷惑。

翻译 我只有一盏指路明灯，那就是经验之灯。

3.

修辞 repletion, parallelism

分析 通过前半段 we have... 的反复出现，强调我们过去所做的努力已经不计其数，又通过后半段的 we have been... 的反复，突出这些努力所换来的结果均遭到不公正地对待。前后形成强烈的反差，句式结构又互相呼应形成平行。最终激化人们的情绪，得出下一句的结论 In vain...，表明这一切的努力终将白费。

翻译 先生们，为了阻止这场即将来临的风暴，一切该做的我们都已经做了。我们请愿过，我们抗议过，我们哀求过；我们曾拜倒在英王御座前，恳请他制止国会和内阁的残暴行径。可是，我们的请愿受到蔑视，我们的抗议反而招致更多的暴力和侮辱，我们的哀求被置之不理，我们被轻蔑地从御座边一脚踢开。

4.

修辞 rhetorical question

分析 一连串的 rhetorical questions 表面看来是疑问的形式，但实际上表达的是肯定的意思，答案就在问句之中，并且语气比一般的陈述句更强，更能引发人们的思考。目的是为了强调紧接出现的具有煽动性的结论：Sir, we are not weak if we make a proper use of those means which the God of nature hath placed in our power.（只要我们能妥善地利用自然之神赐予我们的力量，我们就不弱小。）从而鼓舞人们，消除疑虑和恐惧。

翻译（议长先生，他们说我们太弱小了，无法抵御如此强大的敌人。）但是我们何时才能强大起来？是下周，还是明年？难道要等到我们被彻底解除武装，当英国士兵驻扎在每家每户的时候？难道我们犹豫迟疑、无所作为就能积聚起力量吗？难道我们高枕而卧，抱着虚幻的希望，直到敌人捆住了我们的手脚，就能找到有效的御敌之策了吗？

5.

修辞 onomatopoeia

分析 通过 clanking 模仿锁链撞击的声音，唤起人们头脑中自己被锁链囚禁的形象，锁链声在波士顿平原回响，其实就说明战争也蔓延到了此处。警告人们如果不起来战斗就将成为受锁链束缚的奴隶。反过来理解，既然战争已经不可避免，又不想成为奴隶，唯一的出路只有抗争到底。

翻译 退路已经被切断，除非甘受屈辱和奴役！囚禁我们的枷锁已经铸成。叮当的镣铐声已经在波士顿草原上回响。战争已经无可避免——让它来吧！

V. Language and Style

5.1 Language Focus

1. A 考查内容：分词与逻辑主语的一致性
2. B 考查内容：分词与逻辑主语的一致性
3. A 考查内容：分词与逻辑主语的一致性和时态问题
4. B 考查内容：分词与逻辑主语的一致性
5. B 考查内容：分词与逻辑主语的一致性和时态问题

5.3 Style and Tone

A　　C　　D

VI. Exercises

6.1 Vocabulary

1. B　　2. D　　3. E　　4. A　　5. C

6.2 Text Comprehension

1. The orator stresses that they have no way out but to fight; they must fight for freedom and independence.
2. He adopts an active, resolute attitude toward the war. The orator repeats, "Let it come! Let it come!" Since the war is inevitable, it is right to let it come.
3. America is confronted with warlike preparations, which cover their waters and darken their land. British fleets and armies are in battle array, ready to overwhelm the Americans. They are sent over to bind and rivet upon them those chains which the British ministry has been so long forging.
4. The wise men should neither shut their eyes against a painful truth nor listen to the song of that siren till she transforms them into beasts. They ought to see and hear the things which so nearly concern their temporal salvation. Whatever anguish of spirit it may cost, the wise men should be willing to know the whole truth, to know the worst and to provide for it.
5. The writer illustrates clearly that everything that could be done has been done in order to avert the fast approaching war. He advises the gentlemen to abandon their fond hope of peace and reconciliation. He urges the American people to fight for freedom with great determination.

Chapter 5 Passage 2

II. Text Structure

1. D　2. F　3. B　4. E　5. C　6. A

III. Argument Analysis

1. Paragraph 6, 7, and 8 are used to support claim 2. Paine listed three reasons to explain why religious freedom is the foundation of political freedom.

   →claim + reasons

2. Type of evidence: allusion

   The pillar of the cloud existed only in the wilderness. In the nonage of the Israelites. It protected them in their retreat from Pharaoh, while they were destitute of the natural means of defense, for they brought no arms from Egypt; but it neither fought their battles nor shielded them from dangers afterwards.

   →claim + allusions

3. Type of evidence: facts

   The Jewish kings were in point of government as absolute as the Pharaohs. Men were frequently put to death without trial at the will of the Sovereign. The Romans held the world in slavery, and were themselves the slaves of their emperors. The madman of Macedon governed by caprice and passion, and strode as arrogantly over the world as if he had made and peopled it; and it is needless to imagine that other nations at that time were more refined.

   →claim + facts

IV. Rhetorical Analysis

1.

修辞 imagery, metaphor

分析 The description of the portrait creates a bloody mental picture.

翻译 一个浑身沾满孩子鲜血的母亲的画像只适合地狱里的走廊。

2.

修辞 imagery

分析 The direct quotation and the word “vociferate” appeal to our sense of hearing.

翻译 下议院的议员们叫嚷着“你们是为了可靠的收益而战斗”。

3.

修辞 personification

分析 America is given feminine attributes, being portrayed as it is attractive yet vulnerable.

翻译 因此美国必须承受苦难，因为她拥有一些可以失去的东西。她的罪名就是富有。

4.

修辞 contrast

分析 A stark contrast between the low price and huge profit.

翻译 杀死几个，拿走全部。

5.

修辞 contrast, simile

分析 The use of "like" in this example helps to draw the resemblance between laws and arms, for they both defend people.

翻译 好人具有的安宁诱惑着暴徒；而另一方面，诸如法律之类的武器阻碍着侵略者和掠夺者，使其保持敬畏，这些武器还守护着世间的秩序和财富。

6.

修辞 contrast, alliteration

分析 The same first letter of words ("a") in "avarice and ambition" occurs close together and produces alliteration in the sentence.

翻译 因为人心中存在野心和贪婪，弱者会成为强者的猎物。

7.

修辞 enumeration, allusion

分析 Paine describes absolute power by adding monarchs one by one, which helps the audience to get the real understanding of the speaker's ideas.

翻译 犹太国王的统治的专制程度如同法老。在君主的意志下，不经审判就可以轻易处人以极刑。罗马人以奴隶制统治世界，而他们自己，也做着罗马皇帝的奴隶。马其顿的疯子用反复无常和激烈感情来统治国家，傲慢地阔步于世，仿佛他创造了这个世界并使人们居住于此。

8.

修辞 metaphor

分析 This implies that spiritual freedom is the foundation of political liberty.

翻译 精神自由是政治自由的根基。

9.

修辞 allusion

分析 The author briefly and indirectly refers to a historical figure. It is just a passing comment and the writer expects the reader to possess enough knowledge to spot the allusion and grasp its importance in a text.

翻译 每当有形教会受到压迫，政治自由也会随之遭受损害。读一读玛丽和斯图亚特家族的故事吧。

10.

修辞 allusion

分析 "Quixote" refers to a stupid and impractical figure derived from Cervantes's "Don Quixote", a story of a foolish knight and his misadventures. Paine implies that the claim of Lord Sandwich is imaginary.

翻译 这位当代的堂·吉诃德说道，美国人不会斗争的；因此我们将会斗争。

V. Language and Style

5.1 Language Focus

1. C 2. B 3. D 4. B 5. D

5.2 Language Analysis

语法标签 定语从句

分　析 The facility with which they perceive the dark and ignorant are governed, in popish nations, will always be a temptation to the lovers of arbitrary power to adopt the same methods. (dark: *adj.* lacking in education or the knowledge gained from books; with facility: easily, effortlessly)

翻　译 他们意识到在天主教国家里，统治那些蒙昧无知的人轻而易举。这种轻松总会诱惑专制权力的爱好者们采取同样的方法。

5.3 Tone and Style

Paine boldly attacked the enemy by saying "The reign of Satan is not ended; neither are we to expect to be defended by miracles", "They have lost sight of the limits of humanity", "Send but your troops and the prize is ours. Kill a few and take the whole."

VI. Exercises

6.1 Vocabulary

1. acquit	2. battalion	3. horrid	4. ruffian
5. barbarous	6. fortress	7. plunder	
8. C	9. E	10. B	11. G
12. A	13. H	14. F	15. D
16. D	17. B	18. A	19. A

6.2 Text Comprehension

1. C　2. D　3. A　4. A　5. D

6.

The main claims of this speech include that a peace lover should be willing to take up arms in defense of American freedom, and that both spiritual freedom and political liberty should be defended because they are inseparable.

The allusions in this passage have not interfered understanding when skimming because the gist of each paragraph is often clearly presented in the opening sentence while those supporting allusions can be skipped temporarily.

Chapter 5 Passage 3

II. Text Structure

1. the oppressed 2. wait 3. just 4. unjust

III. Argument Analysis

1. We cannot wait to take the action that will gain ourselves equal civil rights.
2. **Reason 1:** Freedom is never voluntarily given by the oppressor; it must be demanded by the oppressed.

   Reason 2: We have waited for more than 340 years for our constitutional and God-given rights. But we still creep at horse and buggy pace toward gaining a cup of coffee at a lunch counter and now we cannot wait.
3. **Evidence for reason 1:** I have yet to engage in a direct action campaign that was "well-timed" in the view of those who have not suffered unduly from the disease of segregation. For years now I have heard the word "Wait!" It rings in the ear of every Negro with piercing familiarity. This "Wait" has almost always meant "Never."

   Evidence for reason 2: 1) You have seen vicious mobs lynch your mothers and fathers at will and drown your sisters and brothers at whim. 2) You have seen hate-filled policemen curse, kick and even kill your black brothers and sisters. 3) You see the vast majority of your twenty million Negro brothers smothering in an airtight cage of poverty in the midst of an affluent society. 4) When you suddenly find your tongue twisted and your speech stammering as you seek to explain to your six-year-old daughter why she can't go to the public amusement park that has just been advertised on television, and see tears welling up in her eyes when she is told that Funtown is closed to colored children, and see ominous clouds of inferiority beginning to form in her little mental sky, and see her beginning to distort her personality by developing an unconscious bitterness toward white people. 5) when you have to concoct an answer for a five year old son who is asking: "Daddy, why do white people treat colored people so mean?" when you take a cross county drive and find it necessary to sleep night after night in the uncomfortable corners of your automobile because no motel will accept you; 6) when you are humiliated day in and day out by nagging signs reading "white" and "colored"; 7) When your first name becomes "nigger," your middle name becomes "boy" (however old you are) and your last name becomes "John," and your wife and mother are never given the respected title "Mrs." 8) When you are harried by day and haunted by night by the fact that you are a Negro, living constantly at tiptoe stance, never quite knowing what to expect next, and are plagued with inner fears and outer resentments; 9) When you are forever fighting a degenerating sense of "nobodiness."

IV. Rhetorical Analysis

修辞 rhetorical question

分析 反问句是修辞手法中的一种，是用疑问的句式，表达肯定的观点。反问句表面看来是疑问的形式，但实际上表达的是肯定的意思，答案就在问句之中。反问的形式比一般的陈述句语气更强，更能引起人们的思考。

翻译 难道种族隔离不是在实际上体现了人类的悲剧性分离、可怕的疏离和骇人的罪愆吗？

V. Language and Style

5.1 Language Analysis

1.

语法标签 表语从句，定语从句

分　析 句子主干为 The only answer that...is that...

翻　译 对此质疑，我唯一的回答便是，伯明翰新的当局就如同一个不愿出发的行人，在行动之前必然需要有人催促他们。

2.

语法标签 定语从句

分　析 句子主干为 Frankly, I have never yet to engage in direct action campaign that...in the view of those who...

翻　译 坦白说，我还一次都没参加过在未曾受过种族隔离之苦的人看来算是"合乎时宜"的直接行动。

3.

语法标签 并列句式的转折结构

分　析 句子主干为 The nation of Asia and Africa are..., while we...

翻　译 亚洲与非洲的各个民族，正以喷气机般的速度去赢得政治独立，我们却还在以老牛破车的步调爬行以争取在便餐柜台上能喝上一杯咖啡。

4.

语法标签 并列结构

分　析 句子主干为 Thus, I can urge men to obey..., and I can urge them to...

翻　译 正因为如此，我能够敦促人们服从 1954 年最高法院的判决，因其在道德上是正确的；我也能够敦促他们不服从种族隔离的法令，因其在道德上是错误的。

VI. Exercises

6.1 Vocabulary

1. A	2. E	3. B	4. C	5. D
6. A	7. B	8. C	9. A	10. D

6.2 Text Comprehension

1. The election of Albert Boutwell cannot change the current situation of segregation.
2. To support the point that civil rights can only be gained voluntarily.
3. Obtain it voluntarily themselves.
4. A just law is a man-made code that squares with the moral law or the law of God. An unjust law is a code that is out of harmony with the moral law. To put it in the terms of St. Thomas Aquinas, an unjust law is a human law that is not rooted in eternal law and natural law. Any law that uplifts human personality is just. Any law that degrades human personality is unjust.
5. To strengthen the idea expressed in this sentence.

Passage 4

II. Text Structure

1. necessary
2. Nature and God
3. specific reasons or causes
4. equal
5. life, liberty, and the pursuit of happiness
6. the consent of the governed
7. abolish it and institute new government
8. repeated injuries/oppressions/usurpations
9. the government
10. the citizens of England
11. political ties/connection/bands
12. independent states

III. Argument Analysis

Supporting detail 1:

The legislative concerns focused on the fact that King George III would not allow them to represent in the Parliament. In addition, he refused to let the colonies have their own meetings or government. Although they lacked any representation, they were still forced to accept the laws given to them. He even refused certain territories protection unless they agreed to no representation. Finally, they accused the King of holding secret meetings off the record where he bullied others to agree with him.

Supporting detail 2:

The judicial concerns addressed the concerns the colonies had with their lack of judicial system. They believed that King George III made the judges dependent upon him and controlled their decision. In addition, he would not allow the colonists to have a trial by jury in the colonies but forced them to go back to England.

Supporting detail 3:

The writers were also fearful of the military action in the colonies. They did not agree with King George III' s decision to keep armed soldiers station in the colonies during times of peace. In addition, the colonies were denied any military action of their own, forcing them to rely on Great Britain for any military protection or concern.

Supporting detail 4:

Finally, the Declaration of Independence addressed the lack of protection by Great Britain.

King George III had cut off their trade with other parts of the world. The colonists had continually asked for help to protect their people on sea or from the Native Americans, and he had refused. He had imposed taxes on them without their consent. Worst of all, he had declared war on them by burning their towns and destroying their people. At the very moment, they were writing the Declaration of Independence, the King was sending more troops to the colonies.

V. Language and Style

5.1 Language Analysis

1.

语法标签 形式主语，不定式并列

分　析 It is *n.* to do sth.

形式主语：it；谓语：is；表语：right & duty

真正主语 = 不定式并列 to throw off... & to provide...

时间状语从句：when a long train of abuses and usurpations, pursuing invariably the same object evinces a design to reduce them under absolute despotism

翻　译 然而，当始终追求同一目标的一系列滥用职权和强取豪夺的行为表明政府企图把人民至于专制暴政之下时，人民就有权也有义务去推翻这样的政府，并为新政府未来的安全提供保障。

2.

语法标签 同位语从句并列

分　析 主语：we；谓语：hold；宾语：these truths；补语：to be self-evident

同位语从句 1：that all men are created equal

同位语从句 2：that they are endowed by their creator with certain unalienable rights

同位语从句 3：that they are among these are life, liberty and the pursuit of happiness

同位语从句 4：that to secure these rights, governments are instituted among them, deriving their just power from the consent of the governed

同位语从句 5：that whenever any form of government becomes destructive of these ends, it is the right of the people to alter or to abolish it, and to institute new government, laying its foundation on such principles and organizing its powers in such form, as to them shall seem most likely to effect their safety and happiness

翻　译 我们认为下述真理是不言而喻的：人人生而平等，造物主赋予他们若干不可让与的权利，其中包括生存权、自由权和追求幸福的权利。为了保障这些权利，人们才在他们中间建立政府，而政府的正当权利，则是经被统治者同意授予的。一旦任何形式的政府对这些目标的实现起破坏作用时，人民便有权予更换或废除它，以建立新的政府。新政府必须建立在这样的原则基础上并按照这样的方式组织其权力机关。如此，人民才会认为它最有可能使他们获得安全和幸福。

3.

语法标签 插入语，分号并列

分　析 并列：...；...

句子1：主语 prudence；谓语 will dictate；宾语从句 that governments long established should not be changed for light and transient causes

句子2：主语 all experience；谓语 hath shown= have shown

宾语从句：that mankind are more disposed to suffer, while evils are sufferable, than to right themselves by abolishing the forms to which they are accustomed

插入语：, while evils are sufferable,

翻　译 若真要审慎的来说，成立多年的政府是不应当由于无关紧要和一时的原因而予以更换的。过去的一切经验都说明，任何苦难，只要尚能忍受，人类还是情愿忍受，也不想为申冤而废除他们久已习惯了的政府形式。

4.

语法标签 分号并列

分　析 并列：...; ...; ...

状语从句：whereby the legislative powers, incapable of annihilation, have returned to the people at large for their exercise

后置定语 incapable of annihilation

分词结构作状语 the State remaining in the meantime exposed to all the dangers of invasion from without and convulsion within

翻　译 他在解散众议院之后，又长期拒绝另选他人，于是这项不可剥夺的立法权便归由人民来行使，致使在这期间，各州仍处于外敌入侵和内部骚乱的种种危险之中。

5.

语法标签 插入语，谓语动词并列，省略

分　析 插入语：therefore, 主语：we；谓语并列：must acquiesce & hold

比较状语从句 as we hold the rest of mankind, enemies in war, in peace friends

省略 we hold the rest of mankind, enemies in war, (and we hold the rest of mankind) friends in peace

翻　译 因此，我们不得不宣布脱离他们，以对待世界上其他民族的态度对待他们。同我交战者就是敌人；同我友好者即为朋友。

6.

语法标签 分号并列

分　析 并列：...; ...; ...

主语 he；谓语 has endeavored to do；宾语 the population of these states

动名词结构并列 obstructing... & refusing... & raising...

翻译 他力图阻止各州增加人口，为此目的，他阻挠外国人入籍法的通过，拒绝批准其他鼓励移民的法律的通过，并提高获得新分配土地的条件。

7.

语法标签 倒装

分　析　nor 位于句首，主谓倒装 we have been

翻　译　我们并不是没有想到我们英国的弟兄。

8.

语法标签　句子并列

分　析　并列：..., and...

句子 1：主语 we；谓语 have appealed to；宾语 their native justice and magnanimity

句子 2：主语 we；谓语 have conjured；宾语 them

翻　译　我们曾恳求用人类天生所赋有的正义感和雅量，念在同种同宗的份上，弃绝这些掠夺行为，因为这些行为难免会使我们之间的关系和来往中断。

9.

语法标签　插入语，宾语从句并列，分号并列，分词结构作状语

分　析　插入语：therefore,

同位语：, the representatives of the United States of America,

主语：we

分词结构作状语 1：assembled

分词结构作状语 2：appealing to the Supreme Judge of the world for the rectitude of our intentions

谓语：do publish and declare

宾语从句 1：that these united colonies are, and of right ought to be free and independent states

宾语从句 2：that they are absolved from all allegiance to the British Crown

宾语从句 3：that all political connection between them and the State of Great Britain, is and ought to be totally dissolved

宾语从句 4：that as free and independent states, they have full power to levy war, conclude peace, contract alliances, establish commerce, and to do all other acts and things which independent states may of right do

翻　译　因此，我们这些在大陆会议上集会的美利坚合众国的代表们，以各殖民地善良人民的名义，并经他们授权，向世界最高裁判者申诉，庄严地宣布并昭告：我们这些联合起来的殖民地现在是而且也应是独立自由的国家；我们对英国王室效忠的全部义务，我们与大不列颠王国之间一切政治联系全部断绝；我们完全有权宣战、缔合、结盟、通商和采取独立国家理应有权采取的一切行动和决策。

5.2 Style and Tone

1. Bray out grievances against King George III: has forbidden, has utterly neglected, has refused, tyrants
2. Personalize the British-American conflict: he, our, their, themselves, us
3. Rationality and reason: self-evident; divine providence: creator

VI. Exercises

6.1 Vocabulary

SECTION 1

1. C	2. A	3. B	4. H
5. F	6. G	7. D	8. E
9. assent	10. suspended	11. endowed	12. relinquished
13. evinces	14. harassed	15. dissolved	16. abdicated

SECTION 2

1. F	2. B	3. D	4. C
5. H	6. G	7. A	8. E
9. plundered	10. levied	11. acquiesce	12. redressed
13. wage	14. ravaged	15. endeavored	16. denounced

6.2 Text Comprehension

1. A

Other nations of the world were the audience of the *Declaration of Independence*. The *Declaration* worked to justify the colonies' break with Britain and to declare that the United States had a right to exist as a free and independent nation.

2. C

In the 18th century, many Americans were influenced by the ideas of the Enlightenment. This intellectual movement emphasized the power of human rationality and guided many to question traditional religious beliefs. Deists believed that God had created the universe and the laws of nature but did not interfere in human affairs.

3. B

The Enlightenment had a great impact on political philosophy of the 17th and 18th century. An example of this is the thinker, John Locke, who argued that humans were born with the right to life, liberty and property. Any attempt to violate these rights was in defiance of natural law. Locke further argued that in the most extreme cases, people would have to right to overthrow governments that failed to respect these rights.

4. AB

In the 17th century, Europe experienced a Scientific Revolution. A key figure was Isaac Newton, who worked to outline the scientific laws which governed the rational operation of the universe. Philosophers, such as David Hume, appealed to reason in order to establish truths that were "self-evident".

5. B

The authors of the *Declaration* struck a balance in their justification of natural rights. Their explanations looked to both self-evident truths discerned by human reason and the fact that the Creator was the source of these rights. The authors referred to these rights as unalienable which means that no king or government could ever legitimately violate them.

6. B

Slavery as an institution contradicted the ideals at the heart of the Declaration, especially its references to the unalienable right of "liberty". Jefferson, who owned thousands of acres of land in Virginia as well as more than a hundred slaves seemed to embody the contradiction, one which he struggled with for the entirety of his life. In 1791, the African-American author and scientist Benjamin Banneker wrote Thomas Jefferson reminding him of the colonial struggle for independence and protesting the injustice of slavery.

7. D

The authors of the *Declaration* very clearly relied on the ideas of author, John Locke. Locke argued that governments were created in order to ensure the security of people's rights. Citizens entered into a contractual agreement to surrender their absolute freedom in exchange for a government that would work to protect their unalienable rights. There are some differences between the philosophy of John Locke and the ideals of the *Declaration*. Locke wrote that humans had unalienable rights to life, liberty and property. The authors of the *Declaration* replaced property with the loftier ideal of "happiness" or the concept that people ought to have the right to freely pursue meaning in their life.

8. C

The largest portion of the *Declaration* is the statement of the colonies' grievances against Britain. The purpose of the grievances was to show how serious British violations of American rights were and why the American Revolution was justified. In this way, the colonists hoped to show that King George's actions merited the extreme step of revolution.

Chapter 5 Passage 5

I. Warm up

1.3 Reading Skills

1.3.1 Skimming

1. A well-constructed union has the tendency to break and control the violence of faction.
2. By faction, the author refers to "a number of citizens, whether amounting to a majority or a minority of the whole, who are united and actuated by some common impulse of passion, or of interest, adversed to the rights of other citizens, or to the permanent and aggregate interests of the community."
3. There are two methods of curing the mischiefs of faction: the one, by removing its causes; the other, by controlling its effects.

II. Text Structure

Paragraph 1

The author discusses the dangers of faction as the central theme in this paragraph.

Paragraph 2

In this paragraph, the author gives a clear definition of faction.

Paragraph 3 & 4

The author continues to explore two ways to eliminate faction: 1) removing its causes, 2) controlling its effects. Then, he proceeds to delineate the two ways to remove the causes of faction: 1) destroying the liberty, 2) giving every citizen the same opinions, the same passions, and the same interests.

Paragraph 5

The author discredits the first method to remove the cause of faction.

Paragraph 6

The author demurs the second method to remove the cause of faction.

Paragraph 7

By disputing the ways to curb causes of faction, the author draws a conclusion that faction is inevitable.

III. Argument Analysis

Paragraph 1

The author introduces the central theme of his argument—faction in the first sentence, and applauds that a well-constructed union's tendency control faction. In further discussion of faction, he uses his friend's opinion on faction, which is claimed "dangerous vice" and is suggested any plan to provide "proper cure" for it.

Then, the author makes a claim that "the valuable improvements made by the American Constitutions on the popular models, both ancient and modern, cannot certainly be too much admired; but it would be an unwarrantable partiality, to contend that they have as effectually the danger on this side, as was wished and expected."

In supporting his claim, he relies on the fact and evidence that "complaints are everywhere heard from our most considerate and virtuous citizens, equally the friends of public and private faith, and of public and personal liberty, that our governments are too unstable, that the public good is disregarded in the conflicts of rival parties, and that measures are too often decided, not according to the rules of justice and the rights of the minor party, but by the superior force of an interested and overbearing majority."

Then he confesses that he wishes those pieces of evidence discussed above find no bases. But facts and evidence do not favor his wish. And he further reveals evidence that "that some of the distresses under which we labor have been erroneously charged on the operation of our governments; but it will be found, at the same time, that other causes will not alone account for many of our heaviest misfortunes; and, particularly, for that prevailing and increasing distrust of public engagements, and alarm for private rights, which are echoed from one end of the continent to the other. These must be chiefly, if not wholly, effects of the unsteadiness and injustice with which a factious spirit has tainted our public administrations."

Paragraph 5

The author claims that "it could never be more truly said than of the first remedy, that it was worse than the disease". To support his claim, he employs an analogy that "liberty is to faction what air is to fire, an aliment without which it instantly expires." He further reasons that "it could not be less folly to abolish liberty, which is essential to political life, because it nourishes faction, than it would be to wish the annihilation of air, which is essential to animal life, because it imparts to fire its destructive agency."

Paragraph 6

In his assessment the second remedy, the author compares it to the first, claiming that "the second expedient is as impracticable as the first would be unwise". He reasons from several levels to support his claim. First, he asserts that "as long as the reason of man continues fallible, and he is at liberty to exercise it, different opinions will be formed." Second, he contends that "as long as the connection subsists between his reason and his self-love, his opinions and his passions will have a reciprocal influence on each other; and the former will be objects to which the latter will attach themselves." Third, he states that "the diversity in the faculties of men, from which the rights of property originate, is not less an insuperable obstacle to a uniformity of interests. The protection of these faculties is the first object of government."

Paragraph 7

By discrediting the two remedies to check the causes of faction, the author claims that "the latent causes of faction are thus sown in the nature of man; and we see them everywhere brought into different degrees of activity, according to the different circumstances of civil society." When substantiating such claim, he reasons that "a zeal for different opinions concerning religion, concerning government, and many other points, as well of speculation as of practice; an attachment to different leaders ambitiously contending for pre-eminence and power; or to persons of other descriptions whose fortunes have been interesting to the human passions, have, in turn, divided mankind into parties, inflamed them with mutual animosity, and rendered them much more disposed to vex and oppress each other than to co-operate for their common good."

To support his claim, he employs a multiple of examples and contrasts "but the most common and durable source of factions has been the various and unequal distribution of property. Those who hold and those who are without property have ever formed distinct interests in society. Those who are creditors, and those who are debtors, fall under a like discrimination. A landed interest, a manufacturing interest, a mercantile interest, a moneyed interest, with many lesser interests, grow up of necessity in civilized nations, and divide them into different classes, actuated by different sentiments and views."

Thus, he draws the conclusion that "the regulation of these various and interfering interests forms the principal task of modern legislation, and involves the spirit of party and faction in the necessary and ordinary operations of the government."

IV. Rhetorical Analysis

1.

修辞 analogy

分析 The author draws an analogy between liberty to faction and air to fire.

翻译 自由于党争，如同空气于火，是一种离开它就会立刻窒息的养料。

2.

修辞 comparison

分析 The author believes that to abolish liberty to curb faction is not less folly to annihilate air to control fire.

翻译 但是如果因为自由会助长党争而废除政治生活不可缺少的自由，这就如同因为空气给火以破坏力而湮灭给予动物生命必不可少的空气同样的愚蠢。

V. Language and Style

5.1 Language Analysis

1.

语法标签 并列句式，同位语从句

分　析 Complaints are everywhere heard from our most considerate and virtuous citizens, equally the friends of public and private faith, and of public and personal liberty, that our governments are too unstable, that the public good is disregarded in the conflicts of rival parties, and that measures are too often decided, not according to the rules of justice and the rights of the minor party, but by the superior force of an interested and overbearing majority.

翻　译 到处可以听到我们最关心而善良的公民以及拥护公众信用和私人信用，公众自由和个人自由的人们抱怨说，我们的政府太不稳定，在敌对党派的冲突中不顾公益，决定措施过于仓促，而且不是根据公正的准则和小党派的权利，而是根据占压倒多数的超级势力的不可抗力。

2.

语法标签 宾语从句，并列句式，原因状语从句，定语从句

分　析 It will be found, indeed, on a candid review of our situation, that some of the distresses under which we labor have been erroneously charged on the operation of our governments; but it will be found, at the same time, that other causes will not alone account for many of our heaviest misfortunes; and, particularly, for that prevailing and increasing distrust of public engagements, and alarm for private rights, which are echoed from one end of the continent to the other.

翻　译 无论我们多么热切地希望这些抱怨毫无根据，但是现有的证据不容我们否认这些抱怨在某种程度上是成立的。的确，在认真反思我们的情况时会发现，我们遭受的某些痛苦，曾被错误地归咎于政府的工作，但同时也会发现，我们也不能把最大的不幸归结到某个单独的原因上，特别是普遍的、与日俱增的对公共服务的不信任和对私人权利的忧虑，这种担心蔓延在世界各处。

3.

语法标签 后置定语，定语从句

分　析 By a faction, I understand a number of citizens, whether amounting to a majority or a minority of the whole, who are united and actuated by some common impulse of passion, or of interest, adversed to the rights of other citizens, or to the permanent and aggregate interests of the community.

翻　译 我理解，党争就是一些公民，不论是全体公民中的多数或少数，团结在一起，被某种共同情感或利益所驱使，反对其他公民的权利，或者反对社会的永久的和集体利益。

4.

语法标签 倒装

分　析 So strong this propensity of mankind to fall into mutual animosities, that where no substantial occasion presents itself, the most frivolous and fanciful distinctions have been sufficient to kindle their unfriendly passions and excite their most violent conflicts.

翻　译 人类互相仇恨的倾向是如此强烈，以致在没有充分机会表现出来时，最琐碎、最怪诞的差别就足以激起他们不友善的情感和最强烈的冲突。

5.2 Style and Tone

1. necessary　2. general　3. specific　4. solidarity
5. impracticable　6. unwise　7. necessity

VI. Exercises

6.1 Vocabulary

1. D　2. F　3. E　4. B
5. H　6. A　7. C　8. G

6.2 Text Comprehension

1. The author delineates two ways to curb the causes of faction: first, by removing liberty, and second, by controlling its effects. The first remedy is unwise because liberty is fundamental to political life. Although it nourishes faction, it would be folly to destroy liberty to check faction. The second remedy is impracticable because it is infeasible to give every citizen to the same opinions, the same passions, and the same interests. The diversity in the faculties of men would prevent them from forming uniform opinions and passions. And the protection of these faculties should be the first object of government. Thus, the author claims that the causes of factions cannot be removed.

2. First, the causes of faction cannot be removed. Second, different opinions concerning religion, government, leaders and many other points divide men into parities, inflame them with mutual animosity, and render them much more disposed to vex and oppress each other than to co-operate for their common good. Worse, various and unequal distribution of property makes factions more common and durable. Therefore, faction is inevitable.

重要历史事件

1. 美国独立战争

参考思路：

正面：英国是殖民地最大的贸易伙伴，尤其是南方地区的种植园区域，其主要经济作物都是出口到英国。

负面：由于后期税务负担不断加剧，殖民地其实成了英国为获得战争胜利的垫脚石；再加上英国对殖民地的经济政治移民政策多加干涉，更让殖民地人民感觉自己的自由被侵犯。

2. 制宪会议与第一次两党制

参考思路：

三权分立即行政、司法、立法的三种国家权力分属于各自独立的三个不同部门。这样一来，总统只是一个国家名义上的最高统治者和行政部门的长官，能够对国家上下的一切事务直接掌管和负责，但是又由于被司法的最高法院（大法官虽然被总统任命，但是需要通过国会的审议以及其地位终身制）和立法的国会（总统提出的议案要经参议院和众议院的通过才算正式立法成功）所钳制，所以很难出现“一言堂”的独裁状况。

3. 南北战争与重建时期

参考思路：

正面：《解放奴隶宣言》使南北战争变成了一场解放黑奴的战斗，并且最终获得了巨大胜利，在整个国家的范围内废除了奴隶制。另外，在战争中，《解放奴隶宣言》对依然叛乱的南方地区的奴隶主阶层造成了致命的打击，让他们“后院起火”，最终无力招架北方军队，极大加速了战争的进程。

负面：当时，“奴隶是主人的财产”的概念在很多地方依然盛行，联邦政府为了获得战争的胜利，突然宣布所有叛乱地区的奴隶全部解放变成自由人，这也被视为对私人财产的侵犯。

4. 进步运动时期和跻身世界强国

参考思路：

正面：由于西部有银矿，农民希望使用银币。实行银本位符合弱势群体的利益，也符合是进步主义的理念。

负面：美国资本主义一直奉行金本位，因为金本位制下汇率波动的幅度很小，汇率相对稳定。

5. 第一次世界大战和大萧条

参考思路：

正面：美国成为“文化的大熔炉”，汇聚了大量的移民，也因为移民智慧的结晶才有了今天的繁荣。《紧急配额法》(*The Emergency Quota Act*）就是对移民最后的宽容。

负面：移民在一战之后激增，反移民主义者或地方主义者（Nativist）出现了反欧情绪，这种情绪一是来自于无法磨灭的战争伤痛，二是由于不同信仰所带来的不同价值观。

6. 第二次世界大战和战后世界

参考思路：

美国：资本主义国家，资产阶级专政，实行资本主义制度，私有制为其根本制度。

苏联：无产阶级专政，实行社会主义制度，公有制是其根本特征。